A History of

WINE

As Therapy

A History of

WINE

As Therapy

By

SALVATORE P. LUCIA, M.D.
UNIVERSITY OF CALIFORNIA SCHOOL OF MEDICINE

With a Foreword by
SANFORD V. LARKEY, M.D.
THE JOHNS HOPKINS UNIVERSITY

J . B . LIPPINCOTT COMPANY
PHILADELPHIA   MONTREAL

Distributed in Great Britain by

Pitman Medical Publishing Company, Limited, London

Library of Congress Catalog Card No. 63-14618
PRINTED IN THE UNITED STATES OF AMERICA

Foreword

D
R. LUCIA has long been known as a medical historian, a distinguished clinician and an ardent proponent of wine, particularly of its beneficial uses to man. Now he has brought together all his varied talents in this fascinating book on the medical uses of wine throughout the ages.

First, he takes us back to the earliest mention of wine-making, then on through the successive civilizations, telling of the natures of the wines produced in various regions and cultures, always emphasizing the role of wine in medicine, either when used alone for its own sake, or when combined with various drugs. Wisely he has kept to a minimum discussion of the general aspects of viticulture and of the use of wine in religious rites and ceremonies. This restraint gives greater emphasis to his central theme. Thus he traces the story of the medical use of wine from Egypt, to ancient India and China, and on to Greece and Rome, showing the importance of wine in the treatment of disease in all of these civilizations.

He tells us how the tradition built up in these classical times was carried on by Arabian and medieval European physicians. He pays particular attention to the works of Arnald of Villanova. He passes over many of the later Renaissance writings on wine, intentionally. These works were based largely on the classical sources, on Arnald and on "The School of Salerno," works he has already described in great detail. Some of the 16th century books, though, do give us interesting sidelights on the customs of the times, as to wine, in their own countries. Thomas Cogan, in his *Haven of Health* (1584), tells us, at some length, which wines were most used in Elizabethan England, and particularly of their medical uses. He was a firm believer in the virtues of wine, but, as a patriotic Englishman, he is rather upset in having to admit that there are no *English* wines. He makes the best of this seeming fault:

But this our Countrie of England for the coldnesse of the Clime wherin it is situate, bringeth no vines to make wine of, though in other things more necessary it far surmounteth all other Countries. So God hath devided his blessings, that one Nation might have need of another, one Countrie might have entercourse with another. But although wine be no necessarie thing (that is to say) such as Englishmen cannot live without, (for there is, and hath bene many a one in this our Realme that never tasted wine) yet is it without doubt a special gift of God.

Chapter XI, Rise and Fall of the Theriacs, is a most interesting essay on a significant phase of polypharmacy. The concluding chapters deal with the modern history of wine: first, the attacks on the use of wine in medicine, resulting in its gradual elimination from the official medical armamentaria and culminating in the Prohibition era; and then a survey of modern studies on the physiologic effects of wine. The latter was the theme of Dr. Lucia's earlier book, *Wine as Food and Medicine* (1954). The last chapter of the present work epitomizes much of the earlier book and extends it by presenting later findings.

In 1568, Dr. William Turner ended his *New book . . . of all Wines* with this prayer:

Now good reader, seeing that almighty God our heavenly father hath given thee this noble creature of wine, so manye wayes profitable to our bodies and mindes, thanke him with all thy heart, not onely for it, but also for that he hath sent learned Physitians to tell thee how, in what measure, and in what time thou should use them, and not use them. . . .

This admonition of Dr. Turner still holds, and so we should now give thanks that, almost four centuries later, another "learned physician," Dr. Salvatore Lucia, carries on the tradition.

Director of the William H. Welch Medical Library
THE JOHNS HOPKINS UNIVERSITY
SANFORD V. LARKEY, M.D.

Introduction

MY INTEREST in the medicinal uses of wine began some thirty-five years ago, while studying the role of this beverage in the cultural history of man. Throughout the historical texts on medicine and pharmacy I frequently encountered allusions to wine. My curiosity aroused, I began collecting these references. Then, as the significance of the grape and its fermented juice in the evolution of the healing arts became not merely curious but impressive, my inquiry developed into a full-fledged bibliographic project.

Meanwhile, following the end of national prohibition in 1933, a number of research studies on alcoholic beverages, including wine, were being undertaken in university laboratories and clinics in the United States. Some of the findings of these studies kindled new medical interest in the pharmacologic, physiologic, and nutritional values of wine. A demand developed within the medical profession for a thorough evaluation of this ancient beverage in accordance with the standards of modern scientific measurement. This led me to compile a text entitled *Wine as Food and Medicine*, published in 1954, which summarized the data then available.

As the significant findings of new research have continued to accumulate during the past several years, it has become increasingly interesting to compare the empirical data recorded over the past many centuries—enveloped though they often are in primitive superstitions, traditions, and folklore—with the measured results of modern scientific experimentation and analysis. With this objective in mind, the present work has been prepared.

To whom may it be of value? As an aspect of medical history not previously traced, it should be informative to students of pharmacology and nutrition; also, to pharmacists, whose profession was founded on the medicated wines; to enologists, who are responsible for preserving the valuable natural constituents of the wines they produce, and to all others who seek knowledge concerning the substance, the uses, and the history of wine. To members of the medical profession in particular, it should be interesting to view in historical perspective the role of wine as a therapeutic agent, and to realize how fundamental an element this beverage has been in the materia medica. In modern medical practice, because of increased longevity, the promotion and maintenance of health and the prevention of disease have transcended the concept of relief of pain and the cure of disease. Knowledge of nutrition—of the influence of food and drink in the evolution or prevention of specific diseases—is now fully as important as knowledge of the drugs employed in treatment when the time for preventive measures has passed. Among the dietary beverages used by man through the centuries, the next in importance to milk has been wine.

An understanding of the biologic, sociologic, and geographic features of modern man's environment has become essential to the physician. The advantages that have come in recent years are not entirely biologic. They are also psychologic and psychobiologic, and in this area wine plays an important part, not only as a nutrient and a medicine, but also for its psycho-pharmacodynamic effects.

During the years of gathering data for this work I have had invaluable help from many of my friends and co-workers. The author acknowledges with deep gratitude the financial assistance of Mr. and Mrs. Winston S. Cowgill and Mrs. Ruth S. Schuman, whose generosity and understanding helped to make this work possible. For their diligent and patient assistance in abstracting and translating from hundreds of volumes and manuscripts, I am especially indebted to Bertha Landauer, Doris Tronson Davis, Dorothy Lowe, Marjorie Hunt, Gerta Wingerd, and Marianne Ohm. As will be seen from the references, I owe a great deal to my many predecessors, and to the publishers who have given me permission to quote from their works. Acknowledgment is also due to the personnel of the Libraries of the University of California at Berkeley, the College of Agriculture at Davis, the Medical Center at San Francisco, and of the National Library of Medicine at Washington, D.C. Without the help of the staffs of those libraries, many important references pertinent to the present inquiry could not have been included. Finally, my appreciation and thanks to my University faculty colleagues and my fellow members of the Society of Medical Friends of Wine for their comments and constructive criticism.

SALVATORE P. LUCIA, M.D.

Contents

tract—Experiments with wine in liver disease—
Hunger, appetite, and obesity—Wine in diabetes
—Wine as a diuretic—The constituents of wine
analyzed—Absorption of alcohol—Alcohol and
emotional trauma.

Illustrations

A History of

WINE

As Therapy

The Oldest of Medicines

I T IS NOT KNOWN when, by fortunate accident, man first discovered that the juice of the grape, if allowed to ferment, becomes wine. Nor is there any record of when, upon learning empirically that food and drink possess the power to heal, he began to use wine in the treatment of disease. The therapeutic use of wine must have long antedated the oldest inscriptions that depict winemaking, found on the tomb of Ptah-Hotep, who lived at Memphis in northern Egypt about 4000 B.C. While these pictographs document for wine an antiquity of at least 6,000 years, the written record of its medicinal use extends back only some forty centuries. This is enough, however, to establish wine as one of the oldest, perhaps the oldest, of all medicines.

In recent years, with the increasing emphasis on preventive medicine and nutrition, a number of research workers have found renewed interest in wine. They find it significant that this beverage has been usefully employed as a nutritional and therapeutic agent in virtually all countries and in all eras of medical history. They are interested in the medicinal values of wine—which the early physicians knew empirically through centuries of trial and error observations—because some of these values have now been demonstrated in controlled experiments by modern scientists in research centers here and abroad. In this perspective, there is much to be learned in tracing the use of wine in the healing arts from ancient times to the present day.

Most histories of wine are devoted to descriptions of its social, religious, festive, and symbolic uses. For wine has participated universally in the cultural ascent of man, serving as a festive drink at his birth, a solemn drink at his death, a sacred drink in religious ceremonies, and a stimulant of discussion in symposia and intellectual colloquia. Histories of medicine, too, are replete with references to wine, but mainly to wine serving as a menstruum for other therapeutic substances. Few modern medical historians, however, have dwelt at any length on the values attributed over the centuries to wine itself, or on the extensive therapeutic usages of unmedicated or beverage wine in early civilizations. Their brevity is understandable, because the surviving records of ancient healers consist mostly of their more complicated recipes and treatments, which needed to be recorded in order to be remembered. The simpler prescriptions were not written down.

One reason why the historic role of wine as medicine has not been sufficiently emphasized heretofore may be the fact that healing the sick was for countless centuries largely a prerogative of priests and magicians and therefore was considered primarily a religious practice. Throughout the Sumerian, Babylonian, Egyptian, and early Greek and Hebrew civilizations—a period of some eighteen centuries—both wine and medicine were variously associated with religion and magic. The practice of medicine did not become an independent profession until the Greek physician, Hippocrates of Cos, dissociated science from magic and rejected the concept of diseases as divine.

The ancients attributed supernatural powers to wine. Their attribution may have been related to the blood taboo of primitive peoples, a taboo based on the belief that the vital spirit or soul of animate beings resided in the blood, since it was observed that life vanished when blood was spilled. To taste blood was to allow the spirit of the sacrificed subject to enter the body of the person who partook. Plants were thought to be animate, since they bleed when cut, and a vestige of the blood taboo is found in the expression "blood of the grape." Ancient kings and priests offered wine in libations to the gods, because they held the red fluid to be the blood of beings who had once fought against the deities, the vine having sprung from their rotting bodies. The frenzy of intoxication was explained by the supposition that the spirit of the grape had entered the body of the drinker—that the blood of enemies of the gods had agitated the inebriate.

The blood taboo survives today in both the Bible[1] and the Koran,[2] and the concept of the taboo is current in modern medicine, Freud having emphasized its signifi-

cance in his study of the unconscious. Frazier, in *The
Golden Bough*, summarizes it thus: "Wine, therefore, is
considered on two distinct grounds as a spirit, or containing a spirit; first because as a red juice, it is identified with
the blood of the plant, and second because it intoxicates
or inspires."[3]

In contrast to such profound psychologic associations
is the historic role of wine in many countries as a nutritious food. While wine may be defined, for the present
purpose, as the naturally fermented juice of grapes, it is
chemically a highly complex product; as a dietary liquid,
it is surpassed only by milk. The constituents responsible
for its distinctive character are alcohols, aldehydes, ke-
tones, esters, volatile and non-volatile acids, carbon diox-
ide, nitrogenous compounds, pigments, tannins, sugars,
pectins, glycerols, vitamins, and various inorganic components. This composition marks wine as both food and
medicine. As food, wine supplies fluids, calories, minerals,
vitamins, proteins, and other dietary elements. As medicine, wine may act as an appetite stimulant, stomachic,
tonic, tranquilizer, anesthetic, astringent, antiseptic, vasodilator, diaphoretic, diuretic, and antibacterial agent, in
addition to its age-old use as a universal menstruum for
active therapeutic agents derived from plants. It should
be stated that all foods are medicines, and that many medicines are also foods. Like any food, medicine is beneficial
in proper dosage, and harmful when taken in excess.
Likewise, as the ancient physicians knew, one may cure a
malady by an artful and intelligent dietetic regimen, or
one may induce disease by an improper use of food.[4]

Most ancient wines contained foreign substances, which

were added not only for medicinal purposes but also to make the product more palatable. Natural wine is highly perishable, and the early artisans of wine culture, lacking sanitary methods of vinification and storage, used resins, pitch, and sea water to preserve their wines. When spoilage occurred, they added a wide variety of flavorings to disguise the taste—herbs, spices, gums, and honey. This custom survives in the vermouths and other flavored wines of today. Among the more than two hundred botanical substances used by modern wineries in the flavoring formulas for vermouths are dozens of herbs which were listed in the old Egyptian medical papyri. These materials, historically added to wine, include many of the substances listed in the medical formularies of successive ages. The ancients also found it expedient to concentrate their wines. Later, when ready for use, the thick, often desiccated liquids were diluted with selected waters which were reputed to have special medicinal qualities, and which therefore were collected from seas, springs, and rivers from all parts of the ancient world.

Additives to wine served another purpose of the early healers: like many modern physicians, the ancients were inclined to embellish their prescriptions with exotic substances, thereby adding to the psychic effects on their patients. The comparison ends abruptly, however, because the early healers, believing that diseases were caused by supernatural forces, added questionable animal substances to the medicinal wines, and administered them with chants, charms, spells, and amulets, presumably to exorcise demons from the bodies of the sick.

Medicated or mulled[5] wines have been prescribed

throughout all the epochs of medicine. The theriacs of Nicander and Mithridates and the panaceas of Dioscorides actually enjoyed their greatest popularity in eighteenth-century Europe. The medicated wine recipes of Galen, the famous second-century Greek physician who practiced in Rome, were preserved in the Byzantine and Arabic periods, and influenced European medicine for hundreds of years. Virtually all of the antidotaria, formularies, and pharmacopoeias of the world have listed various medicated wines continuously since medieval times.

On the other hand, the therapeutic use of unmedicated wine has fluctuated. For example, the ancient Greek physicians were divided into those who used wine therapeutically and those who did not. The Roman and Byzantine periods, in which wine was the universal medicine, were followed by centuries in which Arabic influence predominated, and the use of wine, forbidden by the Koran, was curtailed although not eliminated. The records of monastic medicine, of Anglo-Saxon leechcraft, and of barber-surgery show the extensive use of wine in medieval Europe. Wine, both medicated and pure, had one of its greatest periods of medical popularity during the seventeeth, eighteenth, and nineteenth centuries.

With the spectacular advances of modern experimental medicine, physicians began to demand objective proof of value for each substance used therapeutically. Such evidence as existed for wine lacked the dramatic quality of the claims made for the new pure and synthetic drugs, which became available in increasing numbers; and the use of wine in medical practice declined. After the period of national prohibition in the United States (1920-1933), an entire generation of physicians had lost touch with the medical lore of wine. It was contended that whatever value wine possesses was due solely to its alcoholic content, and wine was finally dropped from the *United States Pharmacopoeia*.

Following the repeal of the Eighteenth Amendment in 1933, many new research programs on the medical and chemical attributes of alcoholic beverages, including wine, were undertaken in this country, and attention was drawn to the work which had continued, uninterrupted, in European countries. It soon became apparent that there are significant, measurable differences between the effects of wine and those of alcohol, and differences in the effects of the various types of wine. Some age-old claims were disproved, but other values attributed to wine by ancient and medieval physicians were strikingly confirmed. Each year, new clinical and laboratory research has produced steadily mounting evidence of the therapeutic importance of this oldest of medicines.

The history of the medicinal uses of wine, as traced more fully in the succeeding chapters, will thus be seen to follow the pathway of other age-old traditions: the art preceding the scientific explanation by thousands of years, and the explanation demonstrating that there was much of value in the regimen of the physicians of antiquity.

BIBLIOGRAPHY

1. Genesis 9: 3-6.
2. Surah V: 3.

3. Frazier, J. G.: *The Golden Bough*. New York, The Macmillan Co., 1935, Vol. III, p. 248.

4. "When more nourishment is taken than the constitution can stand, disease is caused. . . ."—Hippocrates: *Aphorisms, II, XVII*. Trans., W. H. S. Jones, Loeb Classical Library, London, William Heinemann, Ltd., 1929, Vol. IV, p. 113.

5. The addition of heat or flavoring agents to wine constitutes mulling, from the Latin *mollio* (I soften).

In the Time of Ancient Egypt

THE OLDEST physically preserved record of wine in medicine is that inscribed on a clay tablet excavated in 1910 from the ruins of the ancient Sumerian city of Nippur, south of the supposed site of Babylon. Possibly written by a Sumerian physician interested in recording his more valuable prescriptions, it describes in cuneiform script the compounding of salves from various pulverized medicaments, which in turn were infused with *kushumma* wine. It is estimated that this tablet, now stored in the University of Pennsylvania Museum at Philadelphia, dates from about the end of the third millenium before Christ.[1]

Even older than the Nippur tablet are the wine prescriptions in the principal Egyptian medical papyri, which

although written between 1900 and 1200 B.C., contain
evidence of having been copied in part from earlier medical treatises dating back to 2500 or even to 3400 B.C.

In the Hearst Papyrus (1550 B.C.), wine is specified
in 12 of the 260 prescriptions. Beer is called for in 27,
milk (of cow, ass, or woman who has borne a male child)
in 11, and water in 24.[2] The climates of Egypt and Mesopotamia were more favorable for growing grain than
grapes, and beer consequently was more plentiful than
wine.[3]

Similar recipes are found in the Ebers Papyrus of the
same period, the longest and most famous of such documents. A few poignant examples of its 829 prescriptions
follow:[4]

To eradicate asthma: honey 1 ro [a mouthful], beer 8 ro,
wine 5 ro, are strained and taken in 1 day.

To cause purgation: 6 senna (pods) (which are like beans
from Crete) and fruit of . . . colocynth are ground fine, put
in honey and eaten by the man and swallowed with sweet
wine 5 ro.

To cause the stomach to receive bread: fat flesh 2 ro,
wine 5 ro, raisin 2 ro, figs 2 ro, celery 2 ro, sweet beer 25
ro, are boiled, strained and taken for 4 days.

To expel epilepsy in a man: testicles of an ass are ground
fine, put in wine and drunk by the man; it (i.e., the epilepsy)
will cease immediately.

To treat jaundice: leaves of lotus 4 ro, wine 20 ro, powder
of zizyphus 4 ro, figs 4 ro, milk 2 ro, fruit of juniperus 2 ro,
frankincense ½ ro, sweet beer 20 ro, (it) remains during
the night in the dew, is strained, and taken for 4 days.

Remedy for dejection: colocynth 4 ro, honey 4 ro, are
mixed together, eaten and swallowed with beer 10 ro or wine
5 ro.

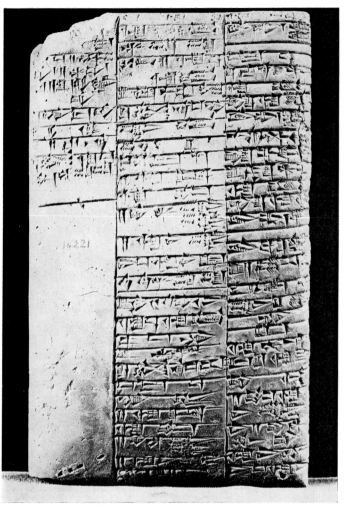

MEDICAL TABLET
FOUND AT NIPPUR
AND DATED ca. 2100 B.C.

Courtesy, University Museum, University of Pennsylvania, Philadelphia, Pennsylvania.

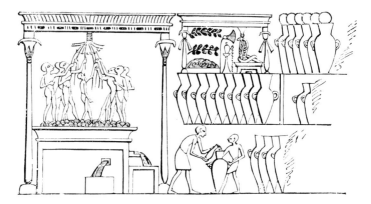

A WALL PAINTING AT THEBES DEPICTING
VARIOUS PHASES OF THE MAKING OF WINE

Large foot press, two vats receiving the issuing juice, the amphorae in which the juice was stored, and the asp—the protecting genius of the storeroom. From Wilkins, J. G.: *Manners and Customs of the Ancient Egyptians*, London, John Murray, 1837, vol. 2, p. 155, illustration No. 141.

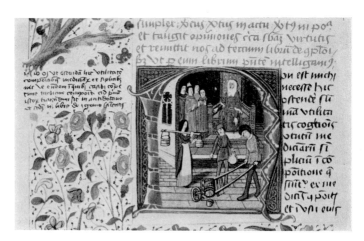

THE CONTROL OF MILK AND WINE

From *Galeni opera varia latine interprete Nicol. de Regio*—Dresden MS. *ca.* 15th century—showing the importance of milk and wine as foods. Courtesy, Koning, D. A. Wittop: *Art and Pharmacy*, Deventer, Holland, The Ysel Press, Ltd., 1957, vol. 1, p. 12.

A good many of the ancient Egyptian prescriptions were rational though empirical. For example, in the recipe for purgation quoted above, both the senna and colocynth [bitter cucumber] are actively cathartic. The following prescription from the London-Leiden Magical Papyrus (third century A.D.) presages the use of "ear-drops" as prescribed by modern physicians for aural discharges:

Medicament for an ear that is watery: Salt, heat with good wine; you apply it after cleansing it first. You scrape salt, heat with wine, and apply it for four days.[5]

In the Coptic papyrus of Meshaîk one prescription of opium, calf's fat, and milk, for earache, admonishes the physician: "The pain will stop immediately. But do not administer this remedy to a man until you have received your fee."[6]

The fact that Egyptian papyri written at dates several centuries apart are often found to contain identical prescriptions suggests that some of the remedies must have accomplished their purpose with regularity. This continuous recording of the therapeutic effects of a preparation constitutes the beginning of pharmacal lore. The numerous botanicals and minerals crudely employed in ancient Egypt, Babylon, and Assyria have served medicine usefully during the many centuries since their introduction. The oil of the castor bean, the seeds of coriander, dill, cumin, caraway and anise; and frankincense, myrrh, opium, salt, sodium carbonate, and the berries of juniper are examples. Many more substances recorded in hieroglyphs remain unidentified because of the enormous difficulties of decipherment.

The bizarre ingredients frequently called for in the

medical papyri—such as goose grease, burnt frog, decayed flesh, the eyes of pigs, the blood of bats, the fat of hippopotami, parts of snakes, urine, vulva of female dog, dung of crocodile, and blood of dragons—are another matter. The references to dragon's blood may have meant cinnabar, red mercuric sulfide, or resin from an East Indian palm tree.[7] It has been suggested that the real reasons for specifying parts of unusual animals were to add mystery and romance, to discourage self-medication, and to protect the business activities of professional healers. Unbeknown to their patients, the healers probably used goose grease universally.[8]

Leake has suggested that the spells, magic incantations, and charms such as the divine cord of seven knots, frequently prescribed together with medicines in the Egyptian papyri, were stage directions to add emphasis to the mystery and to inspire patients' confidence.[9] This may have been the purpose of the following recitation—somewhat wordier than present-day toasts drunk to health—which, according to the Ebers Papyrus, was to be spoken when taking a remedy:

Come remedy! Come thou who expellest (evil) things in this my stomach and in these my limbs! The spell is powerful over the remedy. Repeat it backwards! Dost thou remember that Horus and Seth have been conducted to the big palace at Heliopolis, when there was negotiated of Seth's testicles with Horus, and he shall get well like one who is on earth. He does all that he may wish like these gods who are there. . . . Really excellent, (proved) many times! [10]

It was reasonable for the ancients to resort to magic, since they believed that the sick were possessed by spirits and demons. Each part of the body was associated with a god or goddess by a people whom Juvenal describes as having "divinities springing up in their gardens."[11] Much of the symbolism in Egyptian medicine refers to the eye of the god Horus, son of the beneficent deity, Isis. The eye, gouged out by Seth, the wicked brother of Horus, was restored and healed by the goddess-mother Isis. The frequent allusions to the "green Horus Eye" apparently referred to a spiced wine, hailed as causing good humor even among the gods. The "white Horus Eye" was milk.[12]

The medicinal wines of ancient Egypt were made predominantly of grapes, but some prescriptions, such as the following, called for the more romantic date wine:

To cause a woman to be delivered: date wine, northern salt, oil, are warmed and taken at finger warmth.[13]

In ancient Babylonia, where the grape did not flourish because of the unfavorable soil and climate, wines were made from dates, palm sap, and some even from sesame. For libations to the gods and for special medicinal uses, the Babylonians imported wine from Armenia, Syria, and Lebanon. The mythical explanation for the viticultural failure of Mesopotamia is that the wine god Dionysus, upon learning that the inhabitants drank beer, became angered, turned away from that country, and thereafter denied it his favor.

Although beer was the national drink of Babylonia, the Babylonian medical texts frequently mention *tâbâtu*, a beverage prepared from water and a small addition of the fermented juice of fruits or wine.[14] Presumably grape wine was the ingredient in the following prescription to cure an alcoholic hangover:

If a man has taken too much wine, if his head gives him trouble, if he forgets his words and his speech becomes confused, if his thoughts start wandering and his gaze becomes fixed, to cure him take licorice, . . . beans, oleander . . . and at the approach of the Goddess Gula [that is, in the evening] mix them with oil and wine; let the patient take this potion the next morning before the sun has risen and before anyone has kissed him, and he will recover.[15]

Sacrifices to the gods, required by the polytheistic Babylonian religion, included the ritual use of both wine and beer. Temples were erected on ground that had been consecrated by libations of wine, oil, and honey;[16] and before building a house, the Babylonians sprinkled the foundation with wine.[17]

The complicated recipes of early Egyptian medicine, as recorded in the papyri, refer to wine only as a mixture with other medicaments. Wine and bread, however, are older than any documentary record, and it is known that the Egyptians studied foods and beverages in relation to health. That they also made therapeutic use of beverage wines is implied by the extensive uses of unmedicated wine described in ancient Hebrew and Greek literature, which strongly reflect the influences of Egyptian medicine.

In point of time, the events described in the Old Testament, which presumably occurred after 2000 B.C., were related by word of mouth to succeeding generations and were first written in script sometime before 400 B.C. It has been shown that the medical lore of the Pentateuch, the first five books of Moses, incorporates much that is of Egyptian origin, including references to the Egyptian concept of disease as supernaturally caused, and to healing by magic or miracles. "Moses pored over the medical papyri," writes Charles Brim in *Medicine in the Bible*.[18] In the Biblical narrative of Stephen's defense, it is written: "And Moses was learned in all the wisdom of the Egyptians."[19] Rational medicine, as well as healing by magic, was practiced in Egypt. Moses, reared in the palace of the Pharaoh, had met both magicians and orthodox healers and was qualified to oppose charlatanry, as is expressed in his admonition: "Regard not them that have familiar spirits, neither seek after wizards, to be defiled by them. . . ."[20]

Wine, *Yayin* in Hebrew, is among the few remedies mentioned in the Old Testament. It was used with oil and balsam as an antiseptic or wound dressing; it was both prescribed and prohibited for medical reasons; it was food in liquid form. "Give strong drink unto him that is ready to perish, and wine unto those that be of heavy hearts" is one of the sayings of Lemuel. The following verse, "Let him drink, and forget his poverty, and remember his misery no more," suggests the prescription of wine as a sedative.[21]

Brim offers a direct translation of Psalms 104: 15 from the Hebrew, as follows: "Wine makes empty the heart . . . bread nourishes the heart." He states that the passage refers to the stomach, an organ which the ancient Hebrews allied to the heart. The suggested use of wine to promote appetite is both implied and stated.[22]

"Thy corn, and thy wine, and thine oil" mentioned in the Bible represent health and prosperity. Wine was also classed among the luxuries as "fatness of the earth."[23]

Wine is variously described in the Scriptures as cheering, nourishing, and stimulating. The first text of dietary hygiene is encountered in the Mosaic code. Moses recognized the dangers of improper foods and faulty diet, and advised his wandering people to maintain a strictly regulated and orderly dietary. The early books of the Bible describe in detail the use of wine as an element of ordinary meals and, when embellished, as a supernacular beverage for festive and religious purposes.

Brim interprets the text of the Old Testament as imputing aphrodisiacal qualities to wine, as well as to cucumbers, melons, leeks, onions, and garlic. He also points out that the daughters of Lot used wine to seduce their father.[24] The Talmud provides this description of the effect of wine on a woman: "One glass of wine makes the woman pretty; two glasses and she becomes hateful; at the third glass she lusts invitingly; at the fifth glass she becomes so excited that she will solicit an ass upon the streets."[25]

The medicinal uses of wine are explicitly described in the books of the Talmud, originally written between 536 B.C. and 427 A.D. The chapters bBerakh 35b and bSukka 49b state: "Wine nourishes, refreshes and cheers. Wine is the foremost of all medicines; wherever wine is lacking, medicines become necessary." According to Ned, IX, 8(66b), aged wine is beneficial to the intestines, while new wine is harmful. Unmixed wine is to be drunk after letting blood[26]—a therapeutic practice which has persisted into modern times. There are frequent references to the use of wine as an external application, such as in the ancient rite of circumcision. The ritual, as it is still practiced among the most orthodox Hebrews, requires that after the *mohel* sucks the blood from the cut surface, the wound be bathed with wine, while prayers are chanted for the long life and welfare of the child.[27]

The Babylonian Talmud, as distinct from the Palestinian, mentions the *hiliston*, a sweet and weak new wine; *kushi*, a dark red wine prepared from dark blue grapes; another called "the smoked wine"; and a wine called *oinanthe* (prepared from the wild grape, *Vitis labrusca*), which seems to have been used more generally in medical regimens.[28]

In ancient Persia wine was equally important, and naturally so, since the cultivated grape, *Vitis vinifera*, is supposed to have had its origin there. Poetry and scientific literature, from Herodotus to Omar Khayyám, abundantly documents the Persians' love of wine. (Zoroastrianism, the religion of the Persian kings, did not discourage the drinking of wine, and the modern Iranians appear to be less scrupulous than other Moslems in observing the interdiction of wine as expressed in the Koran.) A play by Epinicus describes King Seleucus drinking wine with barley for relief from the heat.[29] And Xenophon records a speech delivered by Cyrus the Great to his armies on the eve of their departure for the conquest of Babylonia in 539 B.C. It shows that he knew the antiseptic value of wine:

Accordingly, we must put up and carry with us food enough; for without this we should be unable either to fight or to live. As for wine, each one ought to take along only enough to last until we accustom ourselves to drinking water; for the greater part of the march will be through a country where there is no wine, and for that all the wine we can carry will not suffice, even if we take along a very great quantity. That we may not, therefore, fall a prey to sickness when we suddenly find ourselves deprived of wine, we must take this course: let us now begin at once to drink water at our meals, for by so doing we shall not greatly change our manner of living. . . .

So, if after the meal we drink some wine, our soul will lack nothing and find refreshment. But later on we must also gradually diminish the amount taken after dinner, until unconsciously we have become teetotalers. For gradual transition helps any nature to bear changes.[30]

Considerable information on medical practice in ancient times is given by Homer, whose Iliad and Odyssey were first recited about 850 B.C., some three or four centuries after the Trojan War. Homer displays such intimate knowledge of medicine and surgery, especially in his detailed descriptions of battle wounds and their treatment, that many scholars, marveling at his erudition, are inclined to believe that the poet was also a physician.[31]

Throughout the Iliad and the Odyssey, wine is the medicament most frequently mentioned. Homer distinguished between the values of different wines for different medicinal purposes.

Nestor, the wisest of men, offers

. . . wine to the physician Machaon when he was wounded in the right shoulder, although Nestor was a bitter foe of passion; and the wine he gives is Pramnian, too, which we know was heavy and filling . . . and although Machaon has already drunk, Nestor urges him to continue, saying, "Be seated, and drink." He then scrapes some goat's milk cheese over the wine and adds an onion as a relish to make him drink more.[32]

In the writings of Homer, Pramnian wine, often mixed with flour, honey, and milk, was given as a stimulant and as a quencher of thirst. As medicines, acrid wines were always preferred.[33]

In the Lang, Leaf, and Myers translation of the Iliad, Nestor speaks to Machaon as follows: "Sit where thou art, and drink the bright wine, till Hekamede of the fair tresses shall heat warm water for the bath, and wash away the clotted blood."[34] Elsewhere, Ulysses is described as purifying and cleansing his hands, using the Aethiopic, a black strong wine, apparently for its antiseptic qualities.[35]

The Homeric Greeks recognized that the body is sustained by food and drink, for it is told in the Iliad that Athene "in Achilles' breast distilled nectar and pleasant ambrosia, that grievous hunger might not assail his knees."[36] And Achilles is told that "the man who having his fill of food and wine fighteth thus all day against the enemy, his heart [being] of good cheer within him . . ." and his limbs tireless.[37] In the Odyssey, Circe urges Ulysses: "Nay, come, eat ye meat and drink wine, till your spirit shall return to you again."[38] In providing for a voyage, Telemachus is advised by Athene: "make ready corn, and bestow all in vessels, the wine in jars, and barley flour, the marrow of men, in well sewn skins."[39]

The Odyssey tells of Ulysses using acrid or torpid wine to overcome Cyclops in sleep, resting sure that drowsiness or dizziness will result: "When the wine had stolen the wits of the Cyclops . . . the old, taming sleep betook him and from his pharynx he vomited wine."[40] When Circe prepares for Ulysses a potion to induce forgetfulness for his country and relatives, she made it "with

Pramnian wine; but in the food she mixed baneful drugs
that they might utterly forget their native land." [41]

When Helen drugged Telemachus, she used "Ne-
penthe," a powerful Homeric recipe obtained from
Egypt. She "cast a drug into the wine whereof they
drank, a drug to lull all pain and anger, and bring forgetfulness of every sorrow. . . . Medicines of such virtue
and so helpful had the daughter of Zeus, which Polydam-
nia, the wife of Thon, had given her, a woman of Egypt,
where earth the grain-giver yields herbs of greatest
plenty, many that are healing in the cup, and many baneful." [42]

Throughout the Odyssey, Homer describes his war-
riors as carrying wine, water, and corn with them on their
travels, and pouring out libations of wine to the gods
when they were not attending or sacrificing animals.
They apparently had no meals without wine.

From this summary of the available fragments of evidence provided by archaelogy, by translations of the oldest written documents, and by early literature, it appears
that there was widespread therapeutic use of wine in the
time of ancient Egypt. It will be seen in the succeeding
chapters that the influence of wine in medicine in this
early period was carried on to Greece, Rome, medieval
Europe, and ultimately into modern times.

BIBLIOGRAPHY

1. Kramer, Samuel Noah: *From The Tablets of Sumer*. Indian Hills,
Colo., The Falcon's Wing Press, 1956, pp. 56-60, 122. *Kushumma* wine
is not further identified.

2. Leake, Chauncey D.: *The Old Egyptian Medical Papyri*. Lawrence, Kansas, University of Kansas Press, 1952, p. 73.

3. Some mentions of wine in ancient literature refer to fermented juices of fruits other than grapes, and perhaps, in some instances, to fermented grains. *Wine* in this book refers to grape wine; where other fruits are involved, each such material is identified.

4. Ebbell, B.: *The Papyrus Ebers*. Copenhagen, Levin & Munksgaard, 1937.

5. Dawson, Warren R.: *Magician and Leech*. London, Methuen & Co., 1929, p. 122.

6. *Ibid.*: p. 124.

7. Leake: *op. cit.*, p. 45.

8. Dawson: *op. cit.*, p. 66. About goose grease, La Wall, C. H., in *Four Thousand Years of Pharmacy* (J. B. Lippincott Co., 1927) notes that "modern scientific research, as applied to various fats to determine their penetrating power, places goose grease at the top of the list."

9. Leake: *op. cit.*, pp. 55, 65.

10. Ebbell: *op. cit.*, p. 30.

11. *Juvenal: Satire XV, An Egyptian Atrocity*. Trans., G. G. Ramsay. Loeb Classical Library, London, Wm. Heinemann, Ltd., 1940, pp. 289-301.

12. Lutz, H. F.: *Viticulture and Brewing in the Ancient Orient*. Leipzig, J. C. Hinrichs'sche Buchhandlung, 1922, p. 8.

13. Ebbell: *op. cit.*, p. 109.

14. Lutz: *op. cit.*, p. 41.

15. Contenau, Georges: *La Médecine en Assyrie et en Babylonie*. Paris, Librarie Maloine, 1938, p. 195. Gula was the consort of Nineb, the Babylonian god of healing.

16. Lutz: *op. cit.*, pp. 120-121. The Sumerian word *Sabbatu* meant "a day of rest for the heart."

17. Meissner, Bruno: *Babylonien und Assyrien*. Heidelberg, Ethnologische Bibliothek, 1920, Vol. I, p. 275.

18. Brim, Charles J.: *Medicine in the Bible*. New York, Froben Press, 1936, p. ix.

19. Acts 7: 22.

20. Leviticus 19: 31.

21. Proverbs 31: 6, 7. "Strong drink" in the Bible apparently meant heavy wine altered by the addition of piquant, peppery, and highly aromatic substances, such as goat's milk cheese, onion, and other alliaceous roots and bitter substances usually rich in tannin—all of which made the wine taste strong. It did not refer to spirituous liquor, since distillation was unknown to the ancients.

22. Brim: *op. cit.*, p. 113. The Masoretic text reads: "wine that maketh glad the heart of man . . ." and "bread that stayeth man's heart."

23. Deuteronomy 7: 13; Genesis 27: 28.

24. Genesis 19: 30-36.

25. Brim: *op. cit.*, p. 358.

26. Lutz: *op. cit.*, pp. 136, 139.

27. Brim: *op. cit.*, p. 25.

28. Lutz: *op. cit.*, pp. 27-28.

29. Athenaeus: *The Deipnosophists*. Trans., C. B. Gulick. Loeb Classical Library, London, Wm. Heinemann, Ltd., 1927, Vol. IV, p. 432.

30. Xenophon: *Cyropaedia*. Trans., Walter Miller. Loeb Classical Library, London, Wm. Heinemann, Ltd., 1914, Vol. II, pp. 163-165.

31. Ligeros, K. A.: *How Ancient Healing Governs Modern Therapeutics*. New York, G. P. Putnam's Sons, 1937, p. 220.

32. Athenaeus: *op. cit.*, Vol. I, p. 43.

33. Ligeros: *op. cit.*, pp. 227-228. This Pramnian was a vigorous, heavy wine grown on Mount Pramnos in the Island of Icaria, in Lesbos. It was celebrated by Galen and Pliny for its medicinal powers. Aristophanes said of Pramnian wines that they "contract the eyebrows as well as the bowels." (Athenaeus: *op. cit.*, Vol. I, p. 133). On the other hand, Dioscorides mentions a wine called Pramnian, made from the free-run juice of the *Psythian* grape grown in the territory of Smyrna.

34. *The Iliad*. Trans., A. Lang, W. Leaf, and E. Myers. Modern Library ed., Book XVI, p. 250.

35. Ligeros: *op. cit.*, p. 191.

36. *The Iliad, op. cit.*, Book XIX, p. 365.

37. *Ibid.:* pp. 359-360.

38. *The Odyssey*. Trans., S. H. Butcher and A. Lang. Modern Library ed., Book X, p. 158.

39. *Ibid.:* Book II, p. 24.

40. Ligeros: *op. cit.*, pp. 191-192.

41. *Ibid.:* p. 232.

42. *The Odyssey, op. cit.*, Book IV, p. 52.

3

India and the Concept of Soma

INCE MEDICINE in ancient India developed independently of that in Egypt and Mesopotamia, and antedated that of Greece, the use of fermented beverages by the Hindus represents an independent chapter in the history of wine as a therapeutic agent.

In the Vedic period of Indian history (2500 to 200 B.C.), the medicinal values attributed to wine were such that it was actually worshipped as a god. The Aryan conquerors of India were a learned people, and in the healing arts they excelled all other nations of their time. They pioneered in operative surgery; they practiced blood-letting; they prescribed diets, baths, gargles, emetics, enemata, and inhalations. Their materia medica grew eventually to include some 760 medicinal plants, with particular attention directed to aphrodisiacs and to poisons and their antidotes.

Indian medicine was both theurgic and rational. The regimens of treatment included the use of spells and incantations, and basically involved the concept of a deity in liquid form, called Soma. In the Vedas, the most ancient sacred literature of the Hindus, the god-beverage Soma is credited with great medicinal powers. Hymns in its praise are contained in the Rig-Veda, written a thousand or more years before Gautama Buddha taught the doctrine of Buddhism:

> O Soma! you have been crushed, you flow as a stream to Indra, scattering joy on all sides, you bestow immortal food.
> Seven women stir thee with their fingers blending their voices in a song to thee, you remind the sacrificer of his duties at the sacrifice.
> Of all the drinks that Indra have, you are the most pleasant and intoxicating.
> This is Soma, who flows wine, who is strength giving. . . .[1]

In the Rig-Veda, "the god Soma heals whatever is sick," and Soma "makes the blind see and the lame walk."[2] Soma is divine, it purifies, gives health and immortality, and prepares the way to heaven.[3]

Most historians have described Soma as the fermented juice of an East Indian leafless vine (*Asclepias-acida*) of the milkweed family. Its preparation took place in the light of the moon, when the plants were pulled up by the roots and carried to the place of sacrifice on a cart drawn by two goats. A spot covered with grass and twigs was prepared, and the priests crushed the plants with stones and threw them into a woolen sieve of loose weave to bleed. The mass, finally pressed by hand, yielded a fluid which was mixed either with sweet milk, sour milk, or curds and flour; and after nine days the fermentation was completed.[4] This acidulous, slightly astringent juice was the original Soma. At some point in Vedic history, the medicinal powers of Soma became attributed directly to wine, since the Rig-Veda speaks of wine as though it shared alike the powers of Soma.

Most of the Vedic literature applies the term "wine" indiscriminately to a number of alcoholic beverages, including fermentations of honey, molasses, sugar, flowers, roots, leaves, and fruits. The wild grapevine was indigenous to ancient India, while the cultivated variety was introduced from Persia during the early Christian era. In the time of the Rig-Veda, grape wine was imported from Phoenicia, Palestine, Arabia, Italy, and Laodicea in Asia Minor, a fact which establishes the common use of wine in India.[5]

Among the four Vedas, the second—the Atharva-Veda —includes the medical text, Ayur-Veda, which deals with the science of life. Wise, in his *Review of the History of Medicine*, has described the Ayur-Veda as the most ancient system of medicine.[6] The age in which it was written is not known, and only fragments of the original work survive. One of them, the renowned Charaka Samhita, compiled in the second century A.D. from the sixth-century B.C. lectures of Atreya, deals exhaustively with wine, its uses and abuses.

The Charaka Samhita refers to wine as the "invigorator of mind and body, antidote to sleeplessness, sorrow and fatigue . . . producer of hunger, happiness, and digestion . . ."; and states that "if taken as medicine, and not for intoxication, it acts as Amrita [Soma], it cures the natural flow of internal fluids of the body." In another passage, it states: "Wine is natural food but taken indiscriminately produces disease, but when taken properly, it is like Amrita, the immortal drink."[7]

The following ode to wine is found in the Charaka Samhita:

[Wine] who is worshipped with the Gods, invoked in Sautra-moni yajna, who is Amrita to the gods . . . Soma juice to the Brahmans . . . the destroyer of sorrow, fear and anxiety . . . who is pleasure, happiness and nourishment [to men]. . . .[8]

In the Tantras, which belong to the fourth age of the Hindu Shastras (scriptures), five important elements of worship are named; and one among them—wine—is called the god-beverage with the power of Soma: "the Supreme Being in liquid form . . . the great medicine of humanity," which aids in the forgetting of deep sorrows, and is "the cause of great joy . . . the mother of enjoyment and liberation."[9] In Tantric worship wine was indispensable; and following the rise of Buddhism, the Tantric rituals influenced medical thought and practice in Bengal, Nepal, Kashmir, and Gujrat.

The early Hindus, who were advanced in surgery, were among the first to record the use of wine as an anesthetic. An ancient Sanskrit medical text advises:

. . . the patient should be given to eat what he wishes and wine to drink before the operation, so that he may not faint and may not feel the knife.[10]

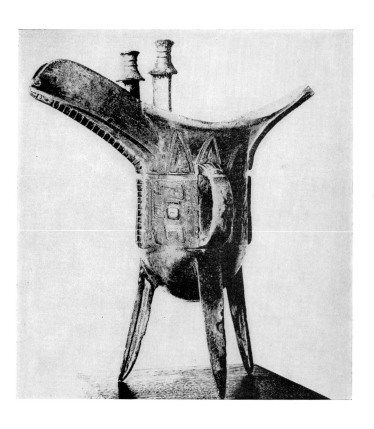

CHÜEH—A LIBATION CUP PROBABLY USED

FOR SCENTED LIQUOR DURING THE SHANG DYNASTY

ca. 1766-1122 B.C.

Courtesy, Staff of the Freer Gallery of Art: *A Descriptive and Illustrative Catalogue of Chinese Bronzes* . . . , Washington, Smithsonian Institution, Oriental Studies No. 3, The Lord Baltimore Press, 1946, p. 24, plate 3.

MEDIEVAL

APOTHECARY SHOP

Woodcut from *Das Buch des Lebens* by Marsilius Ficinus of Florence
(1508). The physician is pointing to jars from whose contents the
dispenser is to prepare medicine. Courtesy, Koning, D. A. Wittop:
Art and Pharmacy, Deventer, Holland, The Ysel Press, Ltd., 1957, vol.
I, p. 13.

The East Indians also used wine in veterinary medicine. The sacred elephants, which represented gods to the Hindus and therefore were the monopoly of kings, were treated with milk for eye inflammations, with the flesh of hogs mixed with *ghee* (clarified butter) for wounds, and with dark wine for other ailments.[11]

The ancient instruction books of the Hindus, the Shastras, mention a number of drinks in common use in the daily life of the people. The *Nagaraka*, man of fashion in ancient India, lived according to strict rules, with a carefully outlined diet that included alcoholic beverages such as *madhu*, made from honey, *maireya* from molasses, and *asava* from sugar; and these were mixed with various sweets, spices, and savories of bitter and acrid taste. Among mild drinks, the *Nagaraka* might partake of water, milk, fresh juices, and sherbets.[12] Another Shastra, the Kama Sutra, describing the duties of a wife, states that wives were allowed only to smell wine, but mistresses were permitted to drink it.[13]

The Smriti, or codes of law, which came into importance in ancient India after the Vedas, forbade the higher castes to use wine. One of the Smriti codes commands that the user of wine should, in punishment, be made to drink it boiling hot.[14] But the great religious epics, the Ramayana and the Mahabharata, praise wine: "Oh, Goddess, be pleased when we come back, we shall propitiate you with a thousand jars of wine."[15] These writings mention that the kings partook of fermented beverages, that wine was used as an offering to the gods, and that sages and hermits used wine in their worship.

Not only did ancient Indian medicine antedate that of

Greece, but it may have influenced the Greeks. At any rate, it is certain that as late as the time of Alexander's Indian expedition in 327 B.C., Hindu physicians and surgeons enjoyed a well-deserved reputation for superior technical knowledge and skill.

The beginnings of Buddhism in the fifth century B.C. did not put an end to the system of Vedic healing, which continued to advance even during the Christian era. But with the Mohammedan conquest in the seventh and eighth centuries A.D., Indian medicine became eclipsed by that of the Moslems, and the religious, sacrificial, and medicinal uses of wine were curtailed.

BIBLIOGRAPHY

1. Bose, D. K.: *Wine in Ancient India.* Calcutta, K. M. Connor and Co., Ltd., 1922, p. 6.
2. Sarma, P. J.: The art of healing in the Rigveda. *Ann. Med. Hist.,* Third Series, 1: 538 (1939).
3. Ragozin, Z. A.: *Media, Babylon, and Persia.* New York, G. P. Putnam's Sons, 1903, pp. 48-49, 52.
4. Bose: *op. cit.,* p. 5.
5. *Ibid.:* pp. 4, 41.
6. Wise, T. A.: *Review of the History of Medicine.* London, J. Churchill, 1867, Vol. I, pp. xxxvii-xxxviii.
7. Bose: *op. cit.,* p. 35.
8. *Ibid.:* pp. 35-36
9. *Ibid.:* pp. 23-24.
10. Jolly, J.: *Indian Medicine.* Trans. from German, supplemented and published by C. K. Kashikar, Poona, 1951, p. 45.
11. *Ibid.:* pp. 20-21
12. Chakladar, H. C.: *Social Life in Ancient India.* Calcutta, Greater India Society, 1929, p. 160.
13. Bose: *op. cit.,* pp. 31-32.
14. *Ibid.:* p. 11.
15. *Ibid.:* p. 15.

4

Wine in Ancient China

ALLUSIONS TO THE USE of wine (*chiu*) abound in the materia medica of the ancient Chinese. Although they refer oftener to fermentations of grains than of grapes, the employment of alcoholic menstruums in Chinese medicine for more than 5,000 years is of sufficient interest here to merit brief review.

The early Chinese healers employed a vast number of therapeutic agents, including ginseng, rhubarb, aconite, opium, arsenic, sulphur, and mercury. In addition, they used many strange ingredients, such as selected parts of animals to which special virtues were attributed. Some of these mixtures are still being sold as Chinese wine tonics.[1]

Bernard Read, in *Chinese Materia Medica*, lists several hundred ancient Chinese prescriptions.[2] A typical recipe called for flesh of the pit viper, prepared by placing the

snake in a gallon of wine, and burying the sealed jar for
one year under a horse's stall. Not more than one pint was
taken as a cure for apoplexy, fistula, stomach or heart
pain, colic, hemorrhoids, worm toxemia, flatulence and
bleeding from the bowel, and miscellaneous other complaints. Another, employing a mixture of lizard's liver,
skin of the cicada locust, and wine, was rubbed on the
navel to produce abortion. Other mystical mixtures included donkey's placenta compounded in wine as a cure
for alcoholism; the liver of a black cat, taken in wine at
midnight, for tuberculosis; the flesh of the macaque mon-
key, pickled in wine, to prevent or cure malaria; and the
excrement of the eagle, ashed and taken with wine, to
dislodge bone obstructions in the throat. A prescription
to cure a heavy cold called for an owl to be smothered
to death, plucked and boiled, its bones charred and taken
with wine.[3]

Nineteen of the eighty-seven formulas in a collection
of ancient and medieval Chinese and Tibetan remedies,
compiled by Franz Hübotter in a study of the pharmacology of eastern Asia, name wine as an ingredient. Examples of these preparations follow:

Effective in heart attack with swelling of extremities, unpleasant coldness of the heart, mental confusion: A solution
consisting of 12 herbs (plants) including such as *Angelica
polymorpha*, zingiber, cinnamon, as well as ground oyster
shells; all of the components are to be dissolved in warm
wine; the patient is to drink this three times a day for 20
days.[4]

To a pregnant woman who has bursting pains in the
region of her waistline, the following should be given on an

empty stomach: *Glycine soja*, previously roasted and boiled, steamed in a large cup of white wine.[5]

In case of post-partum disturbances of the blood causing fainting and mental confusion so that persons cannot be recognized: The patient is to be pulled up into a sitting position by her hair. Put *Zizyphus vulgaris* on hot coals and when it glows throw it into strong vinegar, so that the steam will be inhaled by the patient and revive her. In addition, the following should be given: *Angelica polymorpha*, *Conioselinum univittatum*, heated *Nepeta japonica*, all to be boiled in water, mixed with a good wine and boy's urine. Excellent effect.[6]

In order to promote lactation, take *Saponaria vaccaria*, *Liriope spicata*, and dragon's bones, in a cup of bouillon of pig's feet and a glass of wine. To be taken hot.[7]

The identity and the constituents of some of the wines in the foregoing recipes may be open to question. When distilling was introduced in the thirteenth century, distilled liquors as well as fermentations of grains and of grapes all became classed by the Chinese as wine. And a recipe for making wine, recorded in the *Pei san tsiu kin* (*ca.* 12th century), suggests that the product was less than pure, for it describes the fermentation of grape juice in the presence of sour rice, broth, and leaven, to which apricot kernels were added for flavoring.[8]

On the other hand, Hübotter, who devoted twenty-five years of study in China, specifically identifies the wines to which he refers, as having been made from *Vitis vinifera*, the cultivated grape.[9] He quotes a Chinese book of medicinal prescriptions, printed in the seventeenth century, as stating that this wine, called *p'u-t'ao* in Chinese and *rgun-abrum* in Tibetan, "cures the cough and cleanses from heat."[10]

That at least some of the wines used in early Chinese medicine were made of grapes is further indicated by the frequent descriptions of wine as red, a color which the Chinese regarded as hateful to evil spirits. During the Chou dynasty (*ca.* 1000 B.C.), red wine was used in sacrifices because its color was associated with blood. Apparently, wine mixed with human blood and bone marrow was drunk in some religious and ceremonial rites.[11]

The difficulty in determining the exact nature of ancient Chinese alcoholic beverages is paralleled in present-day attempts to identify the concoctions, designated as wine, that are imported into this country from Saigon, Formosa, and Hongkong.

Although fermented beverages, including those of grapes, have been in continuous use by the Chinese as vehicles for medications for many centuries, China contributes relatively little to the history of wine as medicine.

BIBLIOGRAPHY

1. During the period of national prohibition in America, Chinese exporters, attempting to convince the United States Government of the medicinal character of their wine tonics, presented documentation supporting their claims, referring to many kinds of animal matter mixed with wine. Among the ingredients listed were the reproductive organs of tiger, deer, and panther; South Chinese sparrow steeped in wine; ground viper, lizards, tiger bones, and urine from the bladder of wild fox. In 1959 the government laboratory received a Chinese wine tonic which was claimed to contain ground vipers as an important ingredient.—Communication to the author from Dwight E. Avis, Director, Alcohol and Tobacco Tax Division, Internal Revenue Service.

2. Read, Bernard E.: *Chinese Materia Medica.* Peiping, in the Peking Natural History Bulletin Series, 1931-37, Vols. I-IX.

3. *Ibid.*

4. Hübotter, Franz: *Chinesisch-Tibetische Pharmakologie und Rezeptur.* Ulm, Haug Verlag, 1957, p. 144.

5. *Ibid.:* p. 161.

6. *Ibid.:* p. 169.

7. *Ibid.:* p. 172. It is interesting to note the direction "to be taken hot." The custom of drinking all beverages hot—the result of many centuries of experience in combating infections conveyed by unboiled water—survives in modern Chinese communities.

8. Laufer, Berthold: *Sino-Iranica.* Chicago, Field Museum of Natural History, Publication 201, 1919, Vol. XV, p. 222.

9. The wild grapevine (*Vitis bryoniaefolia* or *Vitis labrusca*) is native to North China, and there are records of the use of its berries for medicinal purposes. The *Vitis vinifera* was introduced into China in the second century B.C. by Chang Ch'ien, who had learned the art of winemaking in Irania.

10. Hübotter: *op. cit.,* p. 104.

11. Ackerman, Phyllis: *Ritual Bronzes of Ancient China.* New York, The Dryden Press, 1945, pp. 75, 98, 100.

Prescriptions of the Early Greek Physicians

WINE WAS ONE of the principal medicines of ancient Greece. In the Iliad it is recorded that Machaon and Podalirius, the famous physician sons of Asklēpios, the Greek god-physician, administered wine medicinally to the wounded heroes of the Trojan War. Hesiod, who wrote an outline of hygiene and diet in the eighth century B.C., considered the problem of heat fatigue in summer, "when . . . women are most wanton and men are feeblest," and advised the use of the wine of Byblos diluted with three parts of water.[1] Alcaeus of Mytilene, who wrote in the seventh century B.C., described wine as the best remedy for fatigue, distress, pain and sorrow.[2]

Hippocrates of Cos (460-370 B.C.), who introduced

the scientific study and treatment of disease and gave the medical profession its ethical ideals, made extensive therapeutic use of wine. He prescribed it as a wound dressing, as a nourishing dietary beverage, as a cooling agent for fevers, as a purgative, and as a diuretic. He made distinctions among the various types of wine, described their different effects, discreetly directed their uses for specific conditions, advised when they should be diluted with water, and, in addition, stated when the use of wine should be avoided.

In his essay on wounds, Hippocrates said: "No wounds should be moistened with anything except wine unless the wound is in a joint. . . ."[3] Among the cooling drinks proper for the treatment of fevers, he recommended one composed of twenty-five parts of water to one of Thasian wine.[4]

The therapeutics of Hippocrates were based on rational observations of the responses of patients to treatment, and on strict hygienic rules. He made no extravagant claims for wine, but incorporated it into the regimen for almost all acute and chronic diseases, and especially during the period of convalescence. Although he advised against its use in illnesses involving the central nervous system, particularly in meningitis, he suggested that even in this disorder, if fever were absent, enough wine should be added to the water to insure an adequate intake and exchange of fluid. By varying the proportion of water, he tempered the dose of wine to the requirements of the illness and the needs of the patient.

Hippocrates described water as "cooling and moist," and wine he characterized as "hot and dry," and contain-

ing "something purgative from its original substance."
Dark and harsh wines, however, were said to be "more
dry," and to ". . . pass well neither by stool nor by urine,
nor by spittle. They dry by reason of their heat, consuming the moisture out of the body."[5] The latter constitutes
the earliest recorded observation of the biophysiologic
effects of wines excessive in their content of tannin—an
agent which retards the motility and mobility of the
bowel, decreases the production of urine, and suppresses
the flow of salivary and other glandular secretions.

Of other wines used therapeutically, he observed:

Soft dark wines are moister; they are flatulent and pass
better by stool. The sweet dark wines are moister and
weaker; they cause flatulence because they produce moisture.
Harsh white wines heat without drying, and they pass better by urine than by stool. New wines pass by stool better
than other wines because they are nearer the must, and
more nourishing; of wines of the same age, those with bouquet pass better by stool than those without, because they
are riper, and the thicker wines better than the thin. Thin
wines pass better by urine. White wines and thin sweet wines
pass better by urine than by stool; they cool, attenuate and
moisten the body, but make the blood weak, increasing in
the body that which is opposed to the blood. Must causes
wind, disturbs the bowels and empties them. It causes wind
because it heats; it empties the body because it purges; it
disturbs by fermenting in the bowels and passing by stool.
Acid wines cool, moisten and attenuate; they cool and attenuate by emptying the body of its moisture; they moisten
from the water that enters with the wine. Vinegar [sour
wine] is refreshing, because it dissolves and consumes the
moisture in the body; it is binding rather than laxative because it affords no nourishment and is sharp.[6]

This passage of the great Hippocrates epitomizes the

logic of a master mind in its observations of human physiology and of the chemical changes upon which physiologic reactions are dependent. The yeast and unaltered sugar of new wines are irritants of the gastrointestinal tract; white, thin, and acid wines are the more diuretic; wines rich in tannin are antidiarrheic. Thus, in terse phrases, the mechanisms for acceleration and retardation of bowel movement and urinary flow and for hydration and dehydration of the body in relation to the ingestion of grape extractives, acids, tannin, and alcohol, were established for the ensuing centuries.

On the other hand, he said of concentrated wines, pomace wines and musts, that

Boiled-down wine warms, moistens and sends to stool. It warms because it is vinous, moistens because it is nutritious, and sends to stool because it is sweet and moreover boiled-down. Wine from grape-husks moistens, sends to stool and fills with wind, because must also does the same.[7]

As to the types of wine to be used in various diseases, Hippocrates observed the different effects of partially fermented ("sweet"), alcoholic ("vinous"), white, and red wines, of honeyed wine, and of acidulated honey:

The following criteria enable us to decide when in acute diseases we should administer sweet wine, vinous wine, white wine and dark wine, hydromel,[8] water and oxymel.[9] Sweet wine causes less heaviness in the head than the vinous, goes to the brain less, evacuates the bowels more than the other, but causes swelling of the spleen and liver. . . .

As to white vinous wine, most and the most important of its virtues and bad effects have already been given in my account of sweet wine. Passing more readily than the other into the bladder, being diuretic and laxative, it always is in many ways beneficial in acute diseases. . . .

A pale wine, again, and an astringent, dark wine, may be used in acute diseases for the following purposes. If there be no heaviness of the head, if the brain be not affected, nor the sputum checked, nor the urine stopped, and if the stools be rather loose and like shavings, in these and in similar circumstances it will be very suitable to change from white wine.[10]

He concluded this discussion by saying:

Should you suspect, however, in these diseases an over-powering heaviness of the head, or that the brain is affected, there must be a total abstinence from wine. In such cases use water, or at most give a pale-yellow wine, diluted and entirely without odour. After each draft of it give a little water to drink, for so the strength of the wine will affect less the head and the reason.[11]

After Hippocrates these fundamental observations were not again as clearly stated until the time of Galen, six hundred years later.

Hippocrates lived during one of the most productive stages of Hellenic civilization, and contributed his share to the magnificent flowering of intellect, culture, arts, and sciences that marked the Age of Pericles. His teachings influenced medicine for 2300 years. His illustrious contemporaries, Socrates, Plato, and Aristotle—perhaps more oenophilic than the master physician—all gave learned dissertations on the various uses of wine.

Socrates is quoted by Xenophon:

Wine moistens and tempers the spirits, and lulls the cares of the mind to rest, . . . it revives our joys, and is oil to the dying flame of life. . . . If we drink temperately, and small draughts at a time, the wine distills upon our lungs like sweetest morning dew. . . . It is then the wine commits no rape upon our reason, but pleasantly invites us to agreeable mirth.[12]

In the second book of the "Laws," Plato, as advocate, advises abstinence for children, for soldiers on military duty, for presidents and judges, and for those who are about to procreate children, and as philosopher he adds:

. . . that boys shall not taste wine at all until they are eighteen years of age; . . . afterwards they may taste wine in moderation up to the age of thirty, but while a man is young he should abstain altogether from intoxication and from excess of wine; when, at length, he has reached forty years, after dinner at a public mess, he may invite not only the other Gods, but Dionysus above all, to the mystery and festivity of the elder men, making use of the wine which he [Dionysus] has given men to lighten the sourness of old age; that in age we may renew our youth, and forget our sorrows; and also in order that the nature of the soul, like iron melted in the fire, may become softer and so more impressible.[13]

Aristotle, who gave to biologic science the earliest tracts on botany, zoology, comparative anatomy, and physiology, recommended for temperance mulled wines—wines that were embellished with heat and spices—and stated that they were thus made soft and less intoxicating.[14]

Following Hippocrates came a long procession of noted physicians, all of whom made historic contributions to medicine and who wrote of the therapeutic uses of wine. The original writings of Diocles of Carystus, the anatomist (*ca.* 375 B.C.), and his pupil Praxagoras, the Dogmatist, no longer exist, but fragments are quoted by Athenaeus of Naucratis, who wrote an encyclopedic text in the third century A.D., epitomizing the thoughts and actions of his great predecessors and illustrious contemporaries. Athenaeus attributes to Diocles and Praxagoras the observation that "the quality of sweet wine causes it to remain in the hypochondriac regions" to induce salivation.[15]

In the Vatican and in other European collections are preserved early copies of books by Theophrastus of Eresos, the physician who did for botany what Hippocrates had done earlier for clinical medicine. Theophrastus (370-285 B.C.) described a multitude of medicinal plants decocted in wine, with special reference to wines embellished with the floriated aromas of certain petalled plants. In addition he gave recipes for perfumed and honeyed wines and discussed their effects on the sense of taste. In his time a parasitic plant of great medicinal import grew wild in the vineyards and it became crushed with the grapes in certain wines. The plant was identified as the white hellebore, and Theophrastus recommended it, stating that it "makes the wine so diuretic that those who drink it become quite emaciated."[16]

Next came Mnesitheus (320-290 B.C.), a renowned Hippocratic physician of Athens, a member of the orthodox medical sect called *Logikoi*, whose treatise on "Diet and Drink" is extensively quoted in Athenaeus. Mnesitheus wrote of wine: "In medicine it is most beneficial; it can be mixed with liquid drugs and it brings aid to the wounded. . . . While dark wine is most favorable to bodily growth, white wine is thinnest and most diuretic; yellow wine is dry, and better adapted to digesting foods."[17] Thus he anticipated by twenty-two centuries the observations of Morgan that red wines are richest in vitamins, of Carles and Labbé concerning the superior diuretic effect of white wines, and of Althausen that white wine influences the intestinal absorption of Vitamin A.[18]

The center of Greek medicine at Alexandria revolved about Erasistratus (300-260 B.C.), the founder of systematic physiology and the first of a school of "progressive" physicians who became known in subsequent centuries as the Erasistrateans. Their therapeusis consisted of mild laxatives, barley-water, and wine in extremely small doses.[19] The followers of Erasistratus founded the medical school of Smyrna in the first century B.C. in order to propagate the Erasistratean principles which dealt with hygiene, physiology, dietetics, and the use of wine and drugs.

Another Alexandrian practitioner of note was Cleophantus, a physician, surgeon, and gynecologist of great influence, who did much to simplify therapeutics and who later taught the disciples of Erasistratus at Rome. Cleophantus, according to Pliny, "had brought into notice the treatment of diseases by wine."[20] He was famous for his medicinal prescriptions of wine, and for the quantities of cold water which he gave to his patients.[21] Celsus, in commenting on the regimen for tertian and quartan periodic (malarial) fevers, stated that "In this kind of malady, well before the paroxysm . . . [Cleophantus] poured over the patient's head quantities of hot water; and then gave wine."[22] Furthermore, after the febrile paroxysms had subsided, Cleophantus advised the continued use of wine. Under these circumstances it is clear that he prescribed wine first as an alterant and then as a sedative.

Thus it can be seen that the role of wine in Greek medicine progressed from purely empirical use, with theurgic connotations, in the time of Homer, to scientific use by Hippocrates and his successors. In a land of lush vineyards, where wine was a common article of diet for freemen as well as for slaves, its early inclusion in the therapeutic regimen in disease was to be expected. Hippocrates and the Coan physicians were basically preoccupied with the systematization and organization of diagnosis of disease. They observed with great acumen, however, the different physiologic effects of the various types of wine that were in common use. After Hippocrates the combined efforts of Theophrastus, Mnesitheus, Erasistratus, and Cleophantus broadened the art and science of therapeutics. It was they who championed the specific uses of wines, both natural and altered, in the treatment of particular diseases. The teachings of these masterful Hippocratic physicians ushered in the Graeco-Roman period, in which wine became a most important, if not the most important agent of the time.

BIBLIOGRAPHY

1. Hesiod: *Works and Days*. Trans., Hugh G. Evelyn-White, Loeb Classical Library, London, Wm. Heinemann, Ltd., 1914, p. 47.
2. Ligeros: *How Ancient Healing Governs Modern Therapeutics*, *op. cit.*, pp. 278-279.
3. *Die Werke des Hippokrates: Die Wunden*. Edited and trans., Richard Kapferer. Stuttgart, Hippokrates-Verlag Marquardt & Cie., Vol. IV, XXI/32.
4. Barry, Edward: *Observations, Historical, Critical and Medical, on the Wines of the Ancients*. London, T. Cadell, 1775, p. viii.
5. Hippocrates: *op. cit.*, *Regimen in Acute Diseases, II*, Vol. IV, pp. 325-327.
6. *Ibid.:* pp. 327-329.
7. *Ibid.:* p. 329.

8. *Hydromel,* also called *aqua mulsa* and *melikraton,* consisted of honey and spring water boiled down to one-third to prevent decomposition. *Melikraton* is sometimes translated as "wine mixed with honey," and sometimes refers to a drink of honey and milk. Hippocrates prescribed hydromel in cases of fracture where there is continued fever: "do not give an evacuant, but avoid food, solid or fluid, and for drink use water and not wine, but hydromel may be taken." —Hippocrates: *op. cit., On Fractures,* Vol. III, p. 127.

9. *Oxymel* was made from fresh honey, the comb being crushed and boiled to dissolve out the honey, and the residue acidulated with vinegar. Hippocrates used it as a cough syrup.

10. Hippocrates: *op. cit., Regimen in Acute Diseases,* Vol. II, pp. 105-109.

11. *Ibid.:* p. 119.

12. Xenophon: *Banquet.* Trans., A. Cooper, Philadelphia, Spelman, Smith, Fielding, et al., 1852, p. 607.

13. *The Dialogues of Plato.* Trans., B. Jowett, New York, Random House, 1937, Vol. II, pp. 451, 443.

14. Athenaeus: *The Deipnosophists, op. cit.,* Vol. V, p. 25.

15. *Ibid.:* Vol. I, pp. 141, 143.

16. Theophrastus: *Enquiry into Plants and Minor Works On Odours and Weather Signs.* Trans., Arthur Hort, Loeb Classical Library, London, Wm. Heinemann, Ltd., 1927, Vol. II, p. 267.

17. Athenaeus: *op. cit.,* Vol. I, pp. 157, 143.

18. See pp. 196-197, 193, 184-185.

19. Stubbs, S. C. B., and Bligh, E. W.: *Sixty Centuries of Health and Physick.* New York, Paul B. Hoeber, Inc., 1931, p. 72.

20. Pliny: *Natural History.* Trans., J. Bostock and H. T. Riley, London, Henry G. Bohn, 1855, Vol. V, p. 157.

21. *Ibid.:* Vol. IV, footnote 28, p. 302.

22. Celsus: *De Medicina.* Trans., W. G. Spencer, Loeb Classical Library, London, Wm. Heinemann, Ltd., 1935, Vol. I, p. 281.

6

In Graeco-Roman and Byzantine Medicine

THE ASCENDANCY OF ATHENS and Alexandria in ancient medicine ended with the destruction of Corinth in 146 B.C., after which the Greek cities became vassal states of Rome. From Athens, Alexandria, and Asia Minor, many Greek physicians migrated to Rome.

During the early Graeco-Roman period a schism of noteworthy proportions existed among the expatriate Greek physicians: one group prescribing wine and the other denying its usefulness as medicine. Allbutt, in *Greek Medicine in Rome*, states that "there were teetotal doctors, and wine-bibbing doctors," and that "long and acrimonious controversies and vituperations" raged on this issue.[1] The only "teetotaler" whom Allbutt names is Pleistonicus, of the school of Praxagoras in Athens, whose treatise on digestion advised that water was a more proper drink for the stomach than wine.[2] Among the advocates of wine as medicine were such notable Roman physicians as Asclepiades of Bithynia, Hikesios of Smyrna, and Menecrates of Tralles.

Asclepiades (124-40 B.C.), the most prominent of the wine-prescribing physicians, began his studies in Athens and before coming to Rome was a pupil of Cleophantus, the Erasistratean, at Alexandria. He was physician to Cicero, and is generally credited with the establishment of Greek medicine on a respectable footing in Rome. The therapeutics of Asclepiades was based chiefly upon restriction of diet, the prescription of wine, and the use of gentle and graduated exercises in the open air. He capitalized on the hygienic value of bathing, and is said to have invented the shower bath. Asclepiades wrote an essay, "Concerning the Dosage of Wine," in which he discussed the virtues of various kinds of wine, both Greek and Roman.[3] He gave wine to patients with fever and filled his insane patients with it to the point of drunkenness in order to produce sleep. In cases of lethargy, wine was prescribed to excite and awaken the senses.[4]

Menecrates of Tralles, physician to Emperor Tiberius, was called *physikos oinodotes* (natural philosopher who advises the use of wine), and Asclepiades won the nickname of *oinodotes* (giver of wine).[5]

Hikesios, who in the first century B.C. founded the Erasistratean medical school of Smyrna, wrote a treatise on the preparation of wine, *De Conditura vini*, and a book on diet and drugs, which were widely quoted by his contemporaries. He advised the use of wine as medicine, and had great influence on the later wine-prescribing physicians.[6]

A contemporary of Hikesios was Apollonius of Citium (*ca.* 81-58 B.C.), who wrote a treatise on wines and addressed it to one of the Ptolemies of Egypt, recommending for medicinal purposes foreign wines rather than those of the king's own country.[7]

The original writings of Asclepiades, Hikesios, and Apollonius no longer exist. What they taught about wine as medicine is reflected and supplemented in the books of Celsus, Pliny, and Athenaeus of Naucratis, all of whom quote pointedly from the medical lore of these *oinodotades*.

Although the Graeco-Roman physicians produced major advances in anatomy, physiology, and botany, there was a general lull during this period in the scientific approach to the treatment of disease, an approach that had been introduced by Hippocrates. This is understandable, because before the arrival of the Greeks, healing among the Romans had been a mixture of domestic herbal medicine and theurgy. The Romans, a superstitious and polytheistic people, attributed specific diseases to different gods, and performed orgiastic rites for each of them.[8] The popular belief in the efficacy of the often fantastic folk remedies helped to provide the ground on which healing with miraculous cures subsequently prospered.

Origin of the Theriacs

At this time, personalized in the tracts of Nicander of Colophon and King Mithridates VI of Pontus in Asia

Minor, began the strange history of the theriacs, antidotes, and alexipharmics—the panaceas or cure-alls which influenced medicine throughout the western world for more than nineteen centuries.

The theriacs (a term subsequently anglicized to treacle, which eventually became also the English word for molasses) were mainly medicated wines. A curious link between wine as a festive beverage and wine as medicine is the similarity between the early theriacs, the vermouths, and other flavored wines of today. In fact, most of the spices, herbs, roots, and leaves in present-day formulas for vermouth are found named in the original recipes for the medicated wines of antiquity. The major role of the theriacs during ancient, medieval, and modern times represents a distinct phase in the historic use of wine as a therapeutic agent.

First to use the terms *theriaca* and *alexipharmaca* was Nicander (190-130 B.C.), a poet, physician, and hereditary priest of Apollo. His verse *Theriaca* was written on the symptoms and treatment of venomous bites and stings of animals; his *Alexipharmaca*, on antidotes against other poisons in food and drink. (Theriac is from *thērion*, a wild beast; later, a venomous serpent. Alexipharmic is from the Greek *alexein*, to ward off.) Nicander's theriac included wild thyme, trefoil seed, aniseed, fennel seed, parsley, and meal of vetch, kneaded with the best wine procurable, and made into lozenges, which were to be taken steeped in wine.[9]

After Nicander came King Mithridates (*ca.* 132-63 B.C.), whose "true medicine," mithridatium, was sold in the pharmacies of ancient Rome, later copied by the great

Arabian physicians, then prescribed as a cure for the plague in medieval Europe, and prized by the English as a sovereign remedy for all ills as late as the eighteenth century. To this ancient monarch, modern medicine owes such terms as *mithridatize* and *mithridatism* (immunity from poisons produced by administration of gradually increasing doses).

Mithridates, despite the turmoil of many wars with the Romans, found time to encourage the arts, sciences, and medicine, and had a peculiar fondness for inquiries into deadly poisons, with which he experimented cruelly on his political prisoners. He lived in constant fear of being poisoned, and conceived the idea of immunizing himself by taking small daily doses of baneful drugs. Mithridates was said to have prepared a universal antidote of several dozen ingredients, compounded with honey and taken in wine, which he administered to himself before each dose of poison.[10] His death occurred in 63 B.C. when, routed by Pompey, he poisoned his wife and daughters and then took poison himself. But according to legend, he had immunized himself so successfully that no available drug would affect him; and he had to call in the assistance of a Gallic soldier, who helpfully dispatched the king with a spear. This legend offered effective advertising for the sale of mithridatium in the centuries that followed.

The ingredients of mithridatium varied according to different authors and also with the various editions of their works. Zopyrus (*ca.* 80 B.C.), a Greek physician of Alexandria, devised a formula, which he called Ambrosia, consisting of costmary, male frankincense, white pepper, flowers of round rush, cinnamon, black cassia, Cicilian saffron, myrrh, and Indian nard, which he ground up with boiled honey and dissolved in a draught of wine.

Andromachus the Elder, chief physician to Nero (37-68 A.D.), attained great fame for his mithridatium, which he entitled "Galene." Its seventy-three ingredients included flesh of vipers, opium, rhubarb, black pepper, cinnamon, ginger, cardamoms, and "sealed earth," the latter being a greasy clay with a red tint obtained from oxide of iron, a substance regarded by the ancients as an antidote to all poisons. The formulation of Andromachus was said to "counteract all poisons and bites of venomous animals," and also to "relieve all pain, weakness of the stomach, asthma, difficulty of breathing, phthisis, colic, jaundice, dropsy, weakness of sight, inflammation of the bladder and kidneys, and the plague."[11]

Important though the theriacs were in Graeco-Roman medicine, unmedicated wines, too, were widely employed. It was generally believed among the Romans that new wine (*mustum*), in particular, was healing and non-inebriating. On the festive day in October called the *Meditrinalia*, the special priests of Mars poured an offering of new and old wine to the gods, then tasted some of it for the purpose of being healed, following which they chanted:

> Wine new and old I drink,
> of illness new and old I'm cured.[12]

Sextius Niger (*ca.* 40 A.D.), a disciple of Asclepiades, while shunning the superstitions and magical remedies of the time, advocated the extensive medicinal uses of natural wine.[13]

Celsus, the Encyclopedist

The oldest extant medico-therapeutic document of the Graeco-Roman period is *De re medicina*, written by the Roman encyclopedist, Aurelius Cornelius Celsus (25 B.C.-37 A.D.). It consists of eight books on diseases treated by diet, pharmacals, and surgery. The manuscript, lost until the fifteenth century and rediscovered by Pope Nicholas V, the founder of the Vatican library, was one of the first medical books to be printed (1478). Celsus compiled and annotated the medical writings of Hippocrates, supplemented by contributions made during the four hundred years of the school of Alexandria, and by the works of Asclepiades. His writings encompass a veritable textbook of the therapeutic uses of wine. He prescribed systematically for every disease affecting any part of the body, and most of his medicines included some kind of wine. His text was divided broadly into *Alimenta* and *Medicamenta;* the *Alimenta* dealt specifically with dietetic and hygienic regimen, while wine and its therapeutic attributes were detailed in the *Medicamenta.*

Celsus discussed the relative medicinal values of wines from various viticultural regions of Italy, Sicily, and Greece. Concerning wines of different ages, he stated that "vinegar [soured wine] and that wine which is a few years old, whether dry or rich, are intermediate in quality; and therefore neither of the two ought to be given to weak patients."[14] He classified sweet or salted wine and *mulsum* (must or wine to which honey or various aromatic substances were added) as having laxative effects. He attributed constipating effects to undiluted wine, harsh or resinated, to *mulsum* which had been heated, to *mustum defrutum* (new or unfermented wine which had been boiled down), and to *vinum passum* (raisin wine).[15] Of various wines he wrote: *Vinum passum* was much in demand for invalids; *Mustum defrutum*, when boiled in leaden vessels, was used as an astringent; *Vinum siliatum*, a wine flavored with saxifrage, was usually drunk in the middle of the day; *Vinum posca*, an acidulous drink of sour wine and water, was the ordinary drink of the common people.[16]

Celsus recounted in precise detail the effects of different wines on the digestive tract. Among those that "readily decompose inside" were sweet wine, *mulsum*, *mustum defrutum*, and *vinum passum*. Harsh or resinated wine was listed among foods which "decompose the least within."[17] For stomach ailments he prescribed as follows:

But if anyone suffers from his stomach, he should read out loud, and after the reading take a walk, then exercise himself at handball and at drill or at anything else which brings the upper part of the body into play; on an empty stomach he should not drink water but hot wine; if he digests readily he should take two meals a day; drink light and dry wine, and after a meal drinks should preferably be cold.[18]

Some precautions, however, were noted:

Nor must one absolutely trust those of our patients who when very unwell have conceived a longing for wine or cold water, and in backing up their desires, lay the blame on their perfectly innocent stomach. But those who digest slowly, and whose parts below the ribs on that account become inflated, or who on account of heat of some kind become thirsty at night, may drink before going to bed three or four cupfuls of wine through a fine reed. Also, to counter slow digestion, it is well to read aloud, next to take a walk, then to be either anointed or laved, taking care to drink wine cold, a large drink after dinner, but as I have said through a tube, ending all by drinking cold water.[19]

For its tranquilizing effect in nervous indigestion, Celsus prescribed either full-bodied dry wine or *mulsum:*

It is never expedient to drink wine treated with sea-water, nor indeed thin or sweet wine, but that which is dry and fuller-bodied, and not too old. If one desires to use honeyed wine, it should be made from boiled honey. . . .[20]

In a discussion of jaundice, he recorded that Asclepiades importuned his patients to drink salted water in order that they might be purged. As part of a dietetic regimen in this disease, Celsus prescribed salted Greek wine:

After purgation, for the first three days a moderate amount of food of the middle-class should be taken with salted Greek wine to drink, in order to keep the bowels loose; then on the ensuing three days, food of the stronger class with some meat, keeping to water for drink; next there is a return to the middle class of food, but in such a way that he may be more satisfied therewith, and for drink an undiluted dry wine in place of the Greek; and this diet is varied so that sometimes acrid foods are put in, sometimes the salted wine is again given. . . .[21]

Celsus employed different types of wines in prescriptions for disorders of the eye. In the therapeutic regimen for ophthalmia, he stated:

There should be smeared over the eyeball, of saffron as much as can be taken up in three fingers, of myrrh in amount the size of a bean, of poppy-tears the size of a lentil: these are pounded up in raisin wine, and applied on a probe to the eyeball.[22]

For proptosis he prescribed a salve of Indian nard, poppy-tears, saffron, and fresh rose leaves, mixed up in mild wine. For carbuncles on the outer surface of the eyelid:

. . . the most suitable poultice is one of linseed boiled in honeyed wine, or if that is not at hand, flour boiled in the same.[23]

His prescription for what is currently referred to as a "black eye" reads:

. . . a blow from without at times so injures the eye that it is suffused with blood. . . . In order to relieve inflammation, it is not unfitting to apply a poultice over the injured eye. The best salt from Ammon, or some other salt, is pounded, and oil gradually added until it is of the consistency of strigil scrapings. Then this is mixed with barley-meal which has been boiled in honey wine.[24]

In treatment of the ear, *mulsum* and raisin wine were employed as antiseptics and as menstruums. A typical prescription follows:

. . . for whereas lesions of the eyes keep the mischief to themselves, inflammations and pains in the ears sometimes even serve to drive the patient to madness and death. This makes it more desirable to apply treatment at the very beginning, that there may be no opening for the greater danger. . . . Hot poultices . . . frequently changed, whether composed of fenugreek or linseed or other meal boiled in honey wine, and sponges also wrung out of hot water, applied at intervals, are appropriate. . . . If severe inflammation entirely prevents sleep, there should be added to the poultice half its quantity of toasted and pounded poppy-head rind, and this should be boiled down with the rest in diluted raisin wine.[25]

Maggots in the ear [!] were extracted by an ear scoop, and to prevent their breeding again, a concoction of hellebore and vinegar was used. The dead maggots were flushed out of the ear with a decoction of horehound and wine. Nasal and genital ulcerations were treated likewise.[26]

For swollen but not ulcerated tonsils, Celsus prescribed "that root which they call sweet, crushed and boiled in raisin wine or honey wine," adding directions to anoint the tonsils gently with boiled-down juice of sweet pomegranates, saffron, myrrh, shredded alum, mild wine, and honey. The mixture was to be boiled gently before application. A popular gargle consisted of warm fig and honey wine.[27]

For toothache, he advised that "wine must be entirely cut off," but he permitted an application of the bark of white poplar roots, boiled in diluted wine, to be used for the pain.[28]

Although Celsus listed the recipes for mithridatium and other theriacs, he wrote of them:

Antidotes are seldom needed, but are at times important because they bring aid to the gravest cases. They are appropriately administered for bodily contusions, either from blows or in cases of a fall from a height, or for pain in the viscera, sides, fauces, or internal parts. But they are chiefly necessary against poisons introduced into our bodies through bites or food or drink.[29]

Medicinal Wines of Pliny

Voluminous additional details of the therapeutic uses

of wine in Rome are furnished by Pliny the Elder (23-79 A.D.), who devoted twelve books in his *Natural History* exclusively to medicine. Although the medical writings of Pliny lack the objectivity of Celsus, Pliny displays a wide knowledge of grapes and wine. He mentions nearly two hundred varieties of grapes and lists the names and virtues of 50 *generous* wines, 38 varieties of foreign wines, 7 kinds of salted wines, and 18 varieties of sweet wines.[30] He related wine quality to the proper pruning of grapevines, stating that wine from unpruned vines should not be offered in libations to the gods. Also forbidden for religious purposes were wines from vines "struck by lightning, or near to which a dead man had been hung, or of grapes that have been trodden out by sore feet." Greek wines, too, were excluded from the sacred ministrations, "because they contain a portion of water."[31] Pliny also mentioned distillation, not of wine, which was not distilled until the thirteenth century, but of the "fruit" [resin?] of the cedar, which was boiled and the condensed vapor pressed out from a fleece of wool. The resulting oil was "generally known as *pisselaeon*."[32]

Although he denounced magicians and their trickery and looked with disfavor on the theriacs, Pliny recorded fantastic claims for some medicinal preparations, such as the famous recipe of Democritus for the conception of beautiful and virtuous children. It consisted of ground pine nuts, assorted fruits, honey, myrrh, saffron, yolk of egg, milk, and palm wine.[33] Another example of gullibility is recorded in the description of the *oenotheris* (wine tamer), a wine mixture which "sprinkled upon them has the effect of taming all kinds of animals, however wild."[34]

Like Celsus, whom he occasionally quoted, Pliny ascribed special virtues to *mulsum* (honeyed wine). He said the best was that made with old wine, since honey became incorporated with it more readily than with new or sweet wines, "the mixture of two sweet liquids being in general not attended with good results."[35] When made with astringent wine, or when the honey was boiled, the mulsum did "not clog the stomach." The kind made with boiled honey produced less flatulency, an "inconvenience generally incidental to this beverage." It acted also "as a stimulant upon a failing appetite," and when "taken cold it relaxes the bowels, but used warm it acts astringently."[36] Pliny quoted Varro as saying that jaundice has the name *Regius morbus*, because its cure is effected with honeyed wine.[37] Pliny climaxed his discussion on the virtues of *mulsum* by relating the story of Pollio Romilius, who had lived beyond his hundredth birthday. When asked by his host, Emperor Augustus, how he had retained such vigor of mind and body, Pollio replied: "Honeyed wine within, oil without."[38]

Detailed descriptions occur in Pliny concerning the dilution of wine with water. As to the quantity of water, he said:

. . . that depends entirely upon the strength of the wine; it is generally thought, however, that the best proportions are one cyathus of wine and two of water. If, however, there is a derangement of the stomach, and if the food does not pass downward, the wine must be given in a larger proportion.[39]

He advised water to counteract inebriation:

When drinking wine, it is a very good plan to take a draught of water every now and then; and to take one long draught of it at the last, cold water taken internally having the effect of instantaneously dispelling inebriation.[40]

The fine wines of the ancients, and especially those recommended for medicinal purposes, were concentrated and often required dilution to be palatable. Pliny records that black Maronean wine from the coast of Thrace was sometimes diluted in proportions of one part of wine to eighty of water.

Pliny ascribed curative virtues to salt taken in wine:

Mixed with wine, it [salt] is a gentle aperient to the bowels, and, taken in a similar manner, it acts as an expellent of all kinds of intestinal worms.[41]

He praised a salted medicinal wine named *bion*, which was "administered for its curative qualities in several maladies." It was made from grapes picked before they were quite ripe, then spread out to dry in the hot sun, turned three times daily for three days, and pressed on the fourth day. The juice was placed in casks and left to age in the sun.[42]

Both Pliny and Celsus referred to salt beaten up in wine and honey with meal as a remedy for gout, but their references to gout were not limited to the condition so named today; rather it connoted any pain in the joints of the feet or hands.

Pliny differentiated among many kinds of salt recommended for medicinal uses, and praised especially the salt of Tarentum and that collected from sea foam.[43] He also wrote of a "sea-seasoned" wine made "by placing vessels full of must in the sea, a method which quickly imparts to the wine all the qualities of old age."[44]

As a wash, he advocated rinsing the mouth with wine flavored with anise and bitter almonds:

... it has the effect ... of sweetening the breath, and removing all bad odours from the mouth, if chewed in the morning with smyrnion and a little honey, the mouth then being rinsed with wine.[45]

Pliny had great faith in a wide assortment of herbs and spices administered in various wines. To catmint, which he called "nep," he attributed the power to promote menstrual discharge and to frighten away serpents. Furthermore, he recommended the juice of catmint or a decoction of its root, mixed with myrtle seed and warm raisin wine, as a gargle for quinsy.[46]

He wrote that oil of the berries of black myrtle (*Myrtus communis L.*) make wine

... possess the property of never inebriating. ... This wine, used when old, acts astringently upon the stomach and bowels, cures griping pains in those regions, and dispels nausea.[47]

Saffron in wine, he said, was used to relieve itching sensations and also as a diuretic. When applied with egg, it dispersed all sorts of inflammation, particularly of the eye. "Chaplets, too, [were] made of saffron, and worn on the head," because they were supposed to dispel the effects of wine.[48] One kind of wild marjoram (*O. onites L.*), when taken in white wine, was described as good for stings of spiders and scorpions; and when "applied with vinegar and oil, in wool," it was a "cure for sprains and bruises."[49] Garden thyme boiled in wine was efficacious for the bites of venomous serpents and certain marine animals, and when mixed with wine and applied externally was a sovereign remedy for sciatica.[50]

Bruised leaves of garden rue and wild rue in wine were recommended by Pliny for bites of scorpions, spiders, bees, hornets, wasps, and even of rabid dogs; and, with hyssop, for "gripings of the stomach," arresting internal hemorrhage, nose-bleed and earache, and also as a mouth wash. Pliny stated that in large doses the juice of rue was poisonous, but added, curiously, that its effects were neutralized by hemlock.[51] Rue has always been associated with witchcraft. In modern medicine it has been employed in the treatment of hysteria, worms, and colic, its medicinal properties depending upon the volatile oil it contains.

Dioscorides, Physician to Nero

Another compendium of medicinal wines is found in *De universa medicina*, written about 78 A.D. by Pedacius Dioscorides, who was a Greek army surgeon in the service of Nero. Dioscorides has been called the founder of materia medica because he was the first to write on medical botany as an applied science. His precise descriptions of hundreds of substances, with their dietetic and therapeutic values appended, influenced physicians and pharmacists for sixteen centuries. Dioscorides advised the use of wine for countless ailments, always specifying a particular type. He noted the specific effects of old and new, dry and sweet wines on the nervous system, the digestive tract, the kidneys, and the urinary bladder:

Those wines which are old, are hurters of ye nerves and of the rest of ye senses, yet are they pleasant to ye taste. Wherefore it is to be avoided by those who have any part weake within. Yet for the use of it in health, both a little is taken without hurt, & that diluted in water. But new wine is inflative, hard of digestion, breeding grievous dreams, ureticall. But that which is of a middle age doth avoid either of these evils, wherefore it is to be chosen in ye uses both of health & sickness. . . . the sweet wine doth consist of gross parts & is hard to evaporate, very much puffing up of ye stomach & disturbing of ye belly & ye entrailes, like as the must; yet it doth less inebriate & is convenient for ye bladder & ye kidnies; but ye sharp wine is more ureticall, & a causer both of headache and drunkenness. But ye unripe wine is most fitting for ye digesting of meats, & it is a stopper of ye belly & of other fluxes, but that which is mild doth less touch the sinewy parts, & it is less ureticall. But that made with sea-water is bad for ye stomach, causing thirst, hurting the sinnewes yet good for ye belly, unfitting for such as are late recovered of a sickness.[52]

To a Lesbian wine called *omphakites oinos*, prepared from unripe, dried grapes, Dioscorides attributed the following qualities:

. . . it hath a faculty of binding, is good for ye stomach, & good for lustful women & ye pained in ye small guts, & ye hard of digestion, & ye squeamish-stomached. And it is thought also being supped up to help plaguie affections. But such wines as these are used after many years, for otherwise they are not potable.[53]

For convalescents, he recommended pomace wine, the

thin, weak wine made by adding water to the leftover pulp of grapes after the last-pressed wine is drawn off. Dioscorides and Pliny called it *deuterias oinos, lora, vinum operarium,* or *potimon.*[54] Dioscorides specified its use "for such to whom we doubt to give wine, & yet are compelled to satisfy ye desire of ye sick, & for such as are recovered from sickness that held long."[55] Pliny also mentioned *faecatum,* a wine pressed from grape lees, and added quite correctly that none of these beverages keeps for more than a year.[56]

Dioscorides praised *vinum passum* (raisin wine) and boiled-down wines as nourishing, beneficial in kidney and bladder ailments, and valuable as antidotes for poisons:

Passum which is made of ye sun-dried grape, or dried on the branches, & prest called Creticum, or Protropum, or Pramnium, and that of Must sodden, called Siron or Hepsema, that which is black called Melampsithion is thick, & much nourishing, but ye white is thinner, and that in ye midst hath also a midling faculty. But all are Binding, recalling ye pulse. Being good against all poisons, which kill with exulcerating, when drank with oil, & vomited up again: & against Meconium & Pharicum, & Toxicum & Hemlock & milk curdled in ye stomach, & against ye griefs of ye bladder and kidnies, being corroded & exulcerated: but they are windy, & bad for ye stomach. But that called Melampsithium is properly good for such as have a fluxing belly. But ye white is more mollifying of ye belly than ye other.[57]

Like Celsus and Pliny, Dioscorides attributed special effects to *mulsum* (honeyed wine):

That mulsum is preferred which is made of old & hard wine, & good honey . . . the old is nutritive & that of a middle age, good for ye belly & ureticall. Being taken after meat it hurts, but being drank at ye beginning it fills, but after that it moves ye appetite.[58]

To a *mulsum* called *melikraton*, he ascribed great value as a heart stimulant and as a fine remedy for the relief of bronchial irritation and cough:

Melicrat doth possess ye same force that Mulsum doth. But we use it sodden, for such as we wish to mollify ye belly, or procure vomiting, as for those that have drunk poison, giving it with oil. But we use that which is boiled for such as have feeble pulses, & for ye weak, and coughers, & ye Peripneu-monicall & such as faint with sweating.[59]

A salted honeyed wine, made of an old vintage and with less honey than in *mulsum*, was called *oinos melitites* and was advised in the treatment of long-continued fevers in those with weak stomachs. Dioscorides described it as gently laxative, diuretic and a purge for the stomach, and said it was administered to the "Arthriticall," and the "Nephriticall," and such as had "a weak head."[60]

Dioscorides listed numerous uses for *omphacium*, the juice of unripe grapes allowed to thicken in the sun. It was:

. . . good also for ye Tonsillae, ye uvula, for mouth ulcers, moist flaggy gums, mattery ears, with honey or Passum, but for Fistulas, and old ulcers, and ye Nomas, with Acetum. And it is given for a glister to ye dysentericall, & fluxing women. It is also a sight-quickener. It is good also for ye roughness & ye gnawings of ye corners of ye eyes. It is drank also for ye spitting of blood but lately come, & for that which came by a rupture. But you must use it very well diluted, & but a little of it neither, for it burns mightily.[61]

The dried flowers of the wild grapevine (*Vitis sylvestris*), called *oenanthe*, made into a wine called *oinos oinanthinos* or into an ointment called *oinanthinon*, were prized by Dioscorides:

The virtue of it is binding, whence, being drank it is good for ye stomach & ureticall, stopping ye belly & spitting of blood. Being dried, & smeared on it is effectual for a queazie & sour stomach. Both ye green and ye dry with Acetum [vinegar] & Rosaceum [oil of roses] are a perfusion for ye headache, & it is a Cataplasme of bleeding wounds, keeping them from inflaming, & of beginning Aegilopae [a disease of the eyes], & of ye jaws in ye mouth & of ye Nomae [corroding sores] which are in ye Priuities [Middle English for "Privities", genitals]....[62]

He also attributed medicinal values to the leaves, tendrils, and stalks of grapevines:

The leaves & the tendrils of ye wine-bearing Vine, beaten small and laid on with Polenta [pearl barley], do assuage headaches & ye inflammation & burning of ye stomach & ye leaves (do ye same) being laid on by themselves, they being cooling & binding; & further, ye juice of them being drank, doth help ye dysentericall & ye blood spitters, & ye stomachicall, & women that lust; & the tendrils being macerated in water, and drank, perform ye same things. But the teare of it being like to gum, thickening about the stumps, being drank with wine drives out ye stones (calculi). It heals also ye Lichenas, & Psoras, & Leprosies being anointed on, but you must first rub ye place with nitre. And being often smeared on with oil, it bares the hair, and especially ye moisture that sweats out from a green branch burning, which also being anointed on takes off ye Myrmeciae.[63]

Dried grapes were also recommended by Dioscorides:

Every grape, which is but new-gathered, disturbeth ye belly

and puffeth up ye stomach, but that which hath hanged for some time doth partake but little of these qualities (because that much of ye moisture is dried up), it is good for ye stomach & a recaller of ye appetite & fit for such as are weak. . . . But of ye Uva passa [grapes spread in the sun], ye white is ye more binding, and ye flesh of them being eaten is good for ye arteries [*arteria*: windpipe], and coughs, & ye kidnies, & ye bladder, & for ye dysentery being eaten by itself with the stones, as also being mixed with meal of Milium & of barley & an egg and fried with honey, and so taken . . . .[64]

Historians of medicine frequently quote Dioscorides as the first to mention the employment of mandragora wine for surgical anesthesia and in the cauterization of wounds. Although some maintain that there was no use of anesthetics before the introduction of ether in 1846, since surgical patients in the early years of the art were merely tied down and operations done on them swiftly, Dioscorides had described mandragora and added:

And some do seeth the roots in wine to thirds, & straining it set it up. Using a Cyathus of it for such as cannot sleep, or are grievously pained, & upon whom being cut, or cauterized they wish to make a not-feeling pain . . . but being too much drank it drives out ye life. . . .[65]

Of all the herbs known in antiquity, none has played so great a role in literature as mandrake (*Mandragora autumnalis* Bertol.). It is a poisonous narcotic of the Solanaceae or nightshade family, and was known to the Egyptians, who believed the plant was an aphrodisiac. Legends about the human shape of the root, its frightful shrieks when uprooted, and the necessity of hitching a dog to uproot it because the demon it contained would kill anyone who stood near, are all common features of early English and German folklore, being especially signalized in Shakespeare's *Romeo and Juliet*.[66]

Dioscorides listed mandrake among aphrodisiac drugs, and classified other herbs among the anti-aphrodisiacs. He also listed wormwood (*Artemisia absinthium L.*) as an aphrodisiac, and wrote of wormwood wine (called *absinthites* by Pliny), after which vermouth received its name. The volatile oil of wormwood contains thujone, a narcotic poison, and it is blamed for the dissipations and deaths of absinthe-drinkers during our present century. Absinthe, a French cordial originally flavored with wormwood, is currently prohibited in France and in most countries of the western world.

A contemporary of Pliny and Dioscorides was the Roman agricultural writer, Columella (*ca.* 4 B.C.-65 A.D.), who also emphasized wine as medicine. He discussed the different effects of wines from various grape varieties, and stated that those of the *Apianae vites*, a muscat variety, "yield a sweet wine, but are not good for the head, nerves, and veins." [67]

Wine in the New Testament

The therapeutic values attributed to wine in first century Rome are also reflected in the New Testament. St. Luke the Evangelist, who was a Greek physician of Antioch, echoed the advice of Hippocrates to treat wounds with wine. In Luke 10:30-37 is the story of the Good Samaritan, who upon finding in the road the half-dead victim of an attack by thieves "bound up his wounds, pouring in oil and wine, and set him on his own beast, and brought him to an inn, and took care of him." [68] Luke also discussed old and new wines, quoting Jesus: "No man also having drunk old wine straightway desireth new; for he saith, The old is better." [69] The Apostle Paul, who was educated in the Greek university center of Tarsus, expressed the contemporary medical view of wine when he advised his "son in the faith," Timothy, to "drink no longer water, but use a little wine for thy stomach's sake and thine often infirmities." [70]

In second century Rome, a noted advocate of the therapeutic use of wine was Athenaeus of Attalia, the founder of the Pneumatic school of medicine. He maintained that when carefully used, with attention to proper rules of symptoms and doses, wine arouses the *pneuma* (the vital principle, spirit, or breath) from its torpor and is especially useful in restoring tone to the pulse in fainting and swooning.[71] The teachings of Athenaeus of Attalia were repeated by Archigenes of Apamea and by the celebrated clinician, Aretaeus of Cappadocia (second to third century A.D.), who recommended Italian wines highly, although he does not appear to have visited Rome.[72]

The Wine Therapy of Galen

The greatest Greek physician after Hippocrates was Galen (131-201 A.D.), the founder of experimental physiology, who wrote almost a hundred books, many of which have been preserved. "By him," commented Neuburger, "the healing art of Hippocrates was transformed into the healing science of Galen." [73] Garrison, while criticizing Galen's tendency to boast of miraculous cures, calls him "the most skilled practitioner of his time."[74]

Galen made extensive therapeutic use of wine. He compiled an exhaustive catalogue of vintages from definite areas of the ancient world, delineating their chemical characteristics and physiological effects. He attributed special virtues to wines of great age, stating, for example, that "the Sorrentine begins to be good after twenty-five years" while "the wine of Rhegium which contains more oil than that of Sorrentum, is fit to use after fifteen years." However, of twenty-year-old Falernian, he commented that "any that surpasses this limit induces headache and attacks the nervous system." [75]

Like Hippocrates, whom he revered, Galen maintained that there was no better wound dressing than wine.[76] While serving as a physician to the gladiators, he noted that wounds, when treated with dressings saturated with red wine, did not putrefy. In cases of severe stabbing with evisceration, he bathed the viscera in wine before replacing them in the abdominal cavity; and it has been stated that none of the gladiators died from infected wounds.[77]

In simple cases of fever associated with chills, Galen permitted wine "when the patient is not plethoric," adding:

... it [wine] must be prohibited to those patients who are chilled considerably and are plethoric. . . . Patients suffering from fever due to insomnia or due to an affection of the heart should be put on a humid and succulent regimen, after a bath. Particularly patients subject to insomnia should be given wine freely, unless there are headaches or pulsing in the temples. . . . Also, prescribe wine for the choleric, the sad, or the dreamer; do not give to the irascible until after his passion has subsided.[78]

And he specified light wines in intermittent fevers:

Before the coction of the disease prohibit wine completely; when coction has started give a light wine, diluted and in small quantity; increase the amount as the resolution of the disease approaches. The aliments which humidify and chill are all very useful in legitimate tertian fevers; the quantity of wine given must be that which the patient can digest conveniently . . . very old or naturally warm wines should be prohibited.[79]

For continued fevers, he said:

The wine should be warm and light, as is the wine of Lesbos, in the "flux" of the abdomen; it should be thick, black, and acid in hemorrhages.[80]

In cases of debility and swooning:

If lipothymia [fainting] occurs due to weakness of the stomach orifice, one should apply fortifying cataplasms over this region, those for instance containing dates, wine, *alphiton*, saffron . . . they should be dampened with medicines containing absinthe, olive oil . . . flowers of wild vines, and wine. If the stomach orifice is inflamed . . . and when this organ is weakened, one should give warm wine. If one cannot cause vomiting and relaxation of the stomach with olive oil . . . one should give to drink an infusion of the heads of absinthia in melikraton, then wine. In cases of fainting resulting from heat . . . you will revive the patient by sprinkling over him immediately cold water, fanning him, turning him from side to side and massaging the region of the stomach orifice . . . then you shall give him wine and food. In order to avert syncope it is wise to give food and drink. . . . If you foresee serious troubles you can prevent them by giving wine, particularly wine in which one has put boiled *alica*. . . . Those who become dangerously ill suddenly, to them you should give warm wine with a very small quantity of bread or warm *alica*.[81]

In the discussion of fistulous abscesses, Galen states that:

. . . before applying the agglutinant I am in the habit of cleaning the sinus with wine alone, sometimes with honeyed wine. . . . This wine should be neither sweet nor astringent.[82]

Galen's praise of mithridatium and of other theriacs and antidotes laid the foundations for their popularity during the Middle Ages and as late as the eighteenth century. In the treatise on antidotes, he noted that:

. . . the so-called *theriac antidote* [of Andromachus] . . . is better for viper bites than is mithridatium, although the latter is no less good for other poisons; for some indeed it is better. . . . And if one takes the drug daily, as did our late Emperor Aurelius Antoninus, or Mithridates himself, he will be quite secure against deadly poisons and the drugs called *deleteria* [destructive agents].[83]

In the same book occurs a rather complicated discussion of the wines which should be used in preparing antidotes. As a general rule, Galen advocated that in compounding medicaments for internal use, only pure, strong, unadulterated wines should be employed. He observed that wine could become altered and soured by the action of the substances with which it was mixed, and warned especially against the Tiburtine and Marsian wines for this reason, recommending instead a very old Falernian.

Galen's system of healing was so well organized, so comprehensive, dogmatic, and plausible, that it ruled

European medicine almost until modern times; and his elaborate lists of vegetable drugs, most of them compounded with wine, are to this day called galenicals.

After Galen came Aretaeus the Cappadocian, a clinician who ranked high in the accuracy of his descriptions of diseases. In Book Two of his *Therapeutics of Chronic Diseases*, he gives a classic account of diabetes, in which he describes the maddening thirst and the drying of the body, and in a section describing the cure of the disease, prescribes wine as follows:

Medicines, then, which cure thirst are required, for the thirst is great with an insatiable desire of drink, so that no amount of fluid would be sufficient to cure the thirst . . . .

But the water used as drink is to be boiled with autumn fruit. The food is to be milk, and with it the cereals. . . . Astringent wines to give tone to the stomach, and these but little diluted, in order to dissipate and clear away the other humours; for thirst is engendered by saltish things. But wine, which is at the same time astringent and cooling, proves beneficial by inducing a change and good temperament. . . .[84]

Wine and the Byzantine Physicians

Contributions to scientific knowledge from Rome ended with Galen, and after Constantine transferred his capital to Asia Minor in A.D. 330, Byzantium became the center of Graeco-Roman medicine. Only four medical writers of note appeared during the Byzantine period, and these were mainly compilers, displaying little of the originality characteristic of their predecessors.

Oribasius (325-403), who wrote the *Synagoge* or Encyclopedia of Medicine, is noted chiefly for espousing the teachings of Galen, thereby contributing to Galenic influence during the Dark Ages; and three hundred years later Paul of Aegina (625-690) frankly admitted, in his epitome of medicine, that the ancients had said all that could be said about the subject.

The medical uses of wine at this time are reflected in the *Tetrabiblion* of Aëtius of Amida (502-575), the first Christian physician of note. Aëtius, who had studied at Alexandria, preferred red, slightly astringent wines "for persons in good health, and those who are convalescent from diseases." [85] For the nausea and morbid appetites of pregnant women, particularly those "who are accustomed to live without work," he advised that

They should abstain from sweet foods eaten with bread; they should drink old, tawny, fragrant wine which is a little tart. . . . Further, it is advisable to aid the weak stomach with ointment made from wild grapes, blossoms of the wild pomegranate tree, roses, calyx of the pomegranate blossom, myrtle, leaves of myrrh and fennel seeds applied with wine in the form of a poultice. . . . Further one should put on the stomach dirty woolen or linen rags soaked with wine and oil . . . or nard flavored wine and (ordinary) wine. These drugs ease the gnawing pains of the stomach.[86]

He offered potions for contraception:

Cyrenaic juice (sap) the size of a chickpea, drunk with two ladles full of diluted wine will prevent conception, and will induce the flow. Another: grind equal parts of Cyrenaic sap, rue leaves, opopanax and cover with wax. Take an amount equal to the size of a fava bean (horse bean) and swallow with diluted wine.[87]

In his prescription to cure frigidity in women, he showed deep insight into its psychologic cause:

Indeed we should prescribe strenuous work and offer food which produces warmth (such as) yellow scented old wine, which is barely sweet. Suitable also is wine diluted with sea water.[88]

In a calendar of instructions to sufferers from gout, he advised that the afflicted take, in January, "a glass of pure wine in the morning." [89] After an operation for hypertrophy of the clitoris, he directed that "a sponge wet with astringent wine should be applied, or cold water, especially if there is much tendency to bleeding, and afterwards a sponge with manna or frankincense scattered over it should be bound on." [90] Aëtius used wine in diphtheria, "giving hot wine to drink almost instead of water." [91] He suggested that after tonsillectomy "a mixture of cold water and vinegar be kept in the mouth for some time to prevent the flow of blood" [92] and after external operations "a sponge wet with astringent wine should be applied to the wound." [93]

The only one of the Byzantine compilers who made any original observations of note was Alexander of Tralles (525-605), who contributed descriptions of intestinal worms, insanity, and gout, and also some interesting wine prescriptions. For gray hair he suggested nutgalls in red wine, and for dandruff he recommended rubbing with wine and salves and washing with salt water. A careful student of diseases of the nervous system, Alexander recommended that certain cerebral diseases be treated with narcotics, bleeding, warm baths, and wine.[94]

The fourth, fifth, sixth, and seventh centuries—the Byzantine period—comprised the early Middle Ages, best described as the Dark Ages because of the intellectual stagnation in Europe that followed the decline and final dissolution of the Roman Empire. The work of the Byzantine physicians is valuable principally in that, during the disintegration of the ancient culture and after the destruction of Alexandria in 640 A.D., it was their texts that preserved the best of Greek medicine. Medical science during both the Roman and Byzantine periods was basically Greek, consisting of the Hippocratic teachings supplemented by those of his successors and compiled for later generations by Galen. It also was essentially Greek medicine that prevailed during the Arabic period, and it was Greek medicine that emerged in the centuries following the intellectual reawakening of Western Europe.

BIBLIOGRAPHY

1. Allbutt, Sir T. Clifford: *Greek Medicine in Rome.* London, Macmillan and Co., Ltd., 1921, pp. 154, 330.
2. Athenaeus: *The Deipnosophists, op. cit.,* Vol. I, p. 197.
3. Allbutt: *op. cit.,* p. 330.
4. Cumston, Charles: *History of Medicine.* New York, A. A. Knopf, 1926, p. 119.
5. Allbutt: *loc. cit.*
6. *Ibid.:* pp. 331, 362.
7. Pliny: *Natural History, op. cit.,* Vol. IV, p. 301. Pliny incorrectly attributes this advice to Apollodorus.
8. One of the Roman gods was Liber, deity of fecundity and wine, whose symbol was the phallus. Liber was the early Roman counterpart of the Green Dionysus (Bacchus).
9. Pliny: *op. cit.,* Vol. IV, p. 300.
10. One of the earliest extant formulas for mithridatium is that given by Celsus, who listed among the ingredients costmary, sweet flag, hypericum, gum, sagapenum, acacia juice, Illyrian iris, cardamom, anise, Gallic nard, gentian root, dried rose leaves, poppy-tears, parsley, cassia, saxifrage, darnel, long pepper, storax, castoreum, frankincense, hypocistis juice, myrrh, opopanax, malabathrum leaves, flower of round rush, turpentine-resin, galbanum, Cretan carrot seeds, nard, opobalsam, shepherd's purse, rhubarb root, saffron, ginger, and cinnamon. Celsus: *De Medicina, op. cit.,* Vol. II, p. 57.

11. Thompson, C. J. S.: *The Mystery and Art of the Apothecary*. Philadelphia, J. B. Lippincott Co., 1929, p. 61.

12. Varro: *De Lingua Latina*. Trans., R. G. Kent, Loeb Classical Library, Cambridge, Harvard University Press, 1938, Vol. I, p. 195.

13. Allbutt: *op. cit.*, pp. 375, 378.

14. Celsus: *op. cit.*, Vol. I, pp. 197-199.

15. *Ibid.*: Vol. I, pp. 209-211.

16. *Ibid.*: p. 498.

17. *Ibid.*: pp. 207-209.

18. *Ibid.*: p. 75.

19. *Ibid.*: pp. 75, 77.

20. *Ibid.*: p. 73. Celsus stated that unboiled honey has a laxative effect.

21. *Ibid.*: *op. cit.*, p. 341.

22. *Ibid.*: Vol. II, p. 191.

23. *Ibid.*: p. 205.

24. *Ibid.*: p. 227. The *strigil* was an instrument, grooved like a shoe horn, used by the ancients for scraping the skin at the bath and in the gymnasium. Liquid medicaments were poured into the groove, from which fluid issued in drops. *Ibid.*: p. 228, note b.

25. *Ibid.*: Vol. II, p. 229.

26. *Ibid.*: pp. 51, 237.

27. *Ibid.*: pp. 251-253. The "root called sweet" was liquorice (*Radix dulcis*), which yielded a characteristic sugar (*Loc. cit.*, footnote a, p. 252).

28. *Ibid.*: pp. 247-249.

29. *Ibid.*: p. 55.

30. Pliny: *op. cit.*, Vol. III, pp. 236-251.

31. *Ibid.*: p. 263.

32. *Ibid.*: pp. 288-290.

33. *Ibid.*: Vol. V, pp. 66-67.

34. *Ibid.*: p. 67.

35. *Ibid.*: Vol. III, pp. 246-247.

36. *Ibid.*: Vol. IV, pp. 437-438.

37. *Loc. cit.* Honey is an important element in the modern treatment of jaundice and disorders of the liver. When supplemented with an adequate diet, wine is not contraindicated in disorders of the liver.

38. *Loc. cit.*

39. *Ibid.*: Vol. IV, p. 477.

40. *Ibid.*: p. 473.

41. *Ibid.*: Vol. V, p. 511.

42. *Ibid.*: Vol. III, p. 247.

43. *Ibid.*: Vol. V, p. 512.

44. *Ibid.*: Vol. III, p. 248.

45. *Ibid.*: Vol. IV, p. 270.

46. *Ibid.*: pp. 261-262.

47. *Ibid.*: p. 520.

48. *Ibid.:* p. 370.
49. *Ibid.:* p. 268.
50. *Ibid.:* pp. 376-377.
51. *Ibid.:* pp. 252-256.
52. *The Greek Herbal of Dioscorides.* Englished by John Goodyer A.D. 1655, edited and first printed 1933 by Robert T. Gunther, London, Oxford University Press, 1934, pp. 603-604. Permission to use *The Greek Herbal* is kindly given by the executors of the estate of the late Dr. R. T. Gunther.
53. *Ibid.:* p. 606.
54. *Vinum operarium* meant "laborer's wine." *Potimon* is from potimos, mostly of water. In modern France, pomace wine is called *piquette.*
55. Dioscorides: *op. cit.,* p. 607.
56. Pliny: *op. cit.,* Vol. III, p. 251.
57. Dioscorides: *op. cit.,* p. 604.
58. *Ibid.:* pp. 607-608.
59. *Ibid.:* p. 608.
60. *Loc. cit.*
61. *Ibid.:* p. 603.
62. *Ibid.:* pp. 602-603.
63. *Ibid.:* p. 601.
64. *Ibid.:* p. 602.
65. *Ibid.:* p. 473.
66. Act IV, sc. 3.
67. Columella: *De re rustica.* Trans., H. B. Ash, Loeb Classical Library, Cambridge, Harvard University Press, 1941, p. 243.
68. Luke 10: 34.
69. Luke 5: 39.
70. 1 Timothy 5: 23. Paul and Luke lived in Rome at the same time as Pliny, Dioscorides, and Columella; Paul died about 67 A.D.
71. Allbutt: *op. cit.,* p. 330.
72. *Loc. cit.*
73. Neuburger, Max: *History of Medicine.* London, Oxford University Press, 1910, p. 242.
74. Garrison, F. H.: *An Introduction to the History of Medicine.* Philadelphia, W. B. Saunders Co., 1922, p. 103.
75. Athenaeus: *op. cit.,* Vol. I, pp. 115-119.
76. Allbutt: *op. cit.,* p. 329.
77. Buck, Albert H.: *The Growth of Medicine from the Earliest Times to About 1800.* New Haven, Yale University Press, 1917, p. 163.
78. *Oeuvres de Galien.* Trans., Ch. Daremberg, Paris, J. B. Baillière, 1856, Vol. II, p. 714.
79. *Ibid.:* pp. 724-725.
80. *Ibid.:* p. 734.
81. *Ibid.:* pp. 735-737.
82. *Ibid.:* p. 776.

83. Galen: On Antidotes, in Brock, A. J.: *Greek Medicine*. London, J. M. Dent & Sons, Ltd., 1929, p. 197.

84. *The Extant Works of Aretaeus, the Cappadocian*. Edited and trans. Francis Adams, London, Sydenham Society, 1856, p. 486.

85. *Aetios of Amida*. Trans., James V. Ricci, from the Latin edition of Cornarius, 1542, Philadelphia, The Blakiston Co., 1950, pp. 214-215.

86. *Ibid*.: pp. 21-22. The concept of the prenatal wish associated with the pomegranate is still current in Latin Europe.

87. *Ibid*., p. 25.

88. *Ibid*., p. 57.

89. Freind, J.: *The History of Physick; From the Time of Galen to the Beginning of the Sixteenth Century;* 3rd ed., Part I, London, J. Walthoe, 1726, p. 80.

90. Walsh, J. J.: *Old Time Makers of Medicine*. New York, Fordham University Press, 1911, p. 37.

91. Allbutt: *op. cit.*, p. 410 .

92. *Ibid*.: p. 33.

93. *Ibid*.: p. 37.

94. *Ibid*.: p. 42.

CHAPTER

7

*Wine and the
Arabic Physicians*

AFTER THE DEATH OF MOHAMMED, in
632 A.D., Arabic culture became broadened
and intensified through accelerated studies of
algebra, chemistry, and geology. With the new interests, a
most fruitful era was initiated—the period when alchemists throughout the Moslem empire sought the elixir of
life, laid the foundations for chemical therapeutics, and
broadened the artful practice of medicine. It was an Arabic era in that the language was Arabic and the religion
Islamic, but in reality it was a blend of Greek, Babylonian, and Indian cultures. Greek medicine was predomi-
nant, and this included the extensive therapeutic use of
wine.

Arabic medicine originally came from a heretical

Christian sect, the Nestorians, whose physicians advised wine in the daily diet for the healthy, and prescribed it in numerous recipes for the sick.[1] Before the time of Mohammed the vine grew luxuriantly in northern Arabia and wine was used extensively; but with the spread of the Prophet's teachings the vineyards were destroyed, in some instances at his personal direction.[2] (The Arabic *Gahwah*, meaning wine, later became the word for coffee.)

The Koran forbids the use of wine, which is considered a device of the devil, although it also states that "of the fruits of the date-palm, and grapes, whence ye derive strong drink and good nourishment. . . . [therein] is healing for mankind."[3] The promise of Paradise to "those who have obeyed the Koran" is that they "shall find themselves in a garden of delight. They shall recline in rich brocades upon soft cushions and rugs and be served by surpassingly beautiful maidens, with eyes like hidden pearls. Wine may be drunk there, but 'their heads shall not ache with it, neither shall they be confused. . . .' "[4] In the medieval caliphate capitals of Baghdad, Cairo, Damascus, and Cordova, the juice of the grape flowed abundantly; and the Moslems of liberal tendencies, including those of the present day, have avoided Mohammed's interdiction of wine by making theirs champagne or cognac.

Impelled by the restriction of their religion, the physicians of Islam wrote imposing essays against the evils of intoxication, but at the same time they wrote numerous lengthy tracts on the medicinal values of wine. A few of these authors were Arabians, but most of them came from Persia or Spain, and many were Jewish. They brought to Islam the culture and knowledge of their provenances. One of these men was the famous Persian clinician Rhazes (860-932), who is said to have been the most original of the Moslem physicians. His writings record that he treated wounds with wine, much as Galen did; and Walsh states that

... in wounds in the abdomen, if the intestines are extruded and cannot be replaced, [Rhazes] suggests the suspension of the patient by hands and feet in a bath in order to facilitate their return. If they do not go readily back, compresses dipped in warm wine should be used.[5]

Arabic medical practices of the tenth century are described in the *Almaleki* (Royal Book) of Haly ben Abbas. His encyclopedia of medical knowledge contained a provocative discourse "on the action of natural and artificial wines."[6]

Another Persian, Avicenna (980-1036), the renowned chief physician of the public hospital of Baghdad, wrote a *Canon of Medicine*, which influenced all of Islam and was used as a text-book in the Orient and in the universities of Western Europe until 1650. The *Canon* contains an interesting discussion of wine and its effects, and short essays on its proper and improper uses. Included among the rules concerning the use of water and wine are some which indicate that the author was conversant with Greek and early Roman medical writings, especially those of Galen concerning the virtues of wine, and those of Celsus referable to its specific therapeutic uses. The depth of Avicenna's knowledge and the character of his advice are revealed in the following rules:

800: White light wine is best for those who are in a heated state, for it does not cause headache. . . . It may relieve headache when that is due to heat in the stomach.

802: Wine is beneficial for persons with a predominance of bilious humor, because it gets rid of the excess of this by provoking the urine. . . . The better its aroma (bouquet) and taste, the more beneficial.

Wine is also very efficient in causing the products of digestion to become disseminated through the body.[7]

Discussing old and new wines, he epitomized the views of Dioscorides:

806: As you know, old wine is like a medicine. It is only feebly nutritious. New wine clogs the liver and produces a hepatic "dysentery" by giving rise to much gas.

The best wine to take is that which is clear, white, tending to a red tinge, of good bouquet, and neither tart nor sweet in taste, neither old nor new.[8]

Avicenna was firm in his proscription of wine for children:

735: Wine must not be allowed. . . . because the injurious effect of wine—namely the generation of bilious humour, as is seen in topers—readily influences the child. The advantage in wine is that it excites the secretion of urine, . . . and that it moistens the joints. Neither of these effects is necessary at this age. . . . To give wine to youths is like adding fire to a fire already prepared with matchwood.[9]

For the autumnal years, a more sane and generous prescription was offered, with specific warnings referable to young and sweet wines:

860: The wine which is best for elderly persons is old, red, with warming effect, and diuretic. New and white sweet wine should be avoided, unless a bath is taken after a meal at which such wine is taken, and unless there is thirst. In that case it is allowable to take white wine which is light without much body in it, thus taking the place of plain water. Elderly persons must shun sweet wines which are likely to prove oppilative (but wines prepared with honey may be allowed even in cases where gout is threatened . . .)

Young adults should take it [wine] in moderation. But elderly persons may take as much as they can tolerate. Wine is borne better in a cold country than in a hot one.[10]

Rule 808 deals with the conditions under which alcohol is most rapidly absorbed into the bloodstream:

The wise person will avoid drinking wine when fasting or before the limbs have been refreshed in warm water, or after vigorous exercise.[11]

Avicenna also wrote a knowledgeful dissertation on intoxication and its treatment, for which he was eminently qualified, since it is recorded that he imbibed nightly:[12]

809: Some persons claim that it is an advantage to become intoxicated once or twice a month, for, they say, it allays the animal passions, inclines to repose, provokes the urine and sweat, and gets rid of effete matters. . . . Frequent intoxication breaks down the constitution of the liver and brain, weakens the nerves, and tends to produce diseases of the nervous system, apoplexy, and sudden death.

His advice for over-eager imbibition was as sound then as it is today:

If called to a person who has drunk wine to excess, emesis should be produced as speedily as possible. Failing that he may drink a considerable quantity of water, with or without honey. When emesis has been procured, he should bathe in a full length bath. Then he should be thoroughly rubbed with oil, and left to go to sleep.[13]

The most celebrated Jewish physician of the Arabic world was Rabbi Moses ben Maimon (Maimonides, 1135-1204). A native of Cordova and famous abroad, he ultimately became court physician to Saladin, Sultan of Egypt and Syria. Among his writings is the treatise *De Regimine Sanitatis,* a series of letters on personal hygiene which he wrote for the son of his patron. The son, the Sultan Al Afdal, had complained of poor digestion, and Maimonides outlined a regimen of diet, drink, and exercise, including the following:

Wine is nutritious: It is well known among physicians that the best of the nourishing foods is one that the Moslem religion forbids, i.e., wine. It contains much good and light nourishment. It is rapidly digested and helps to digest other foods. It also removes the superfluities from the pores of the flesh and excretes urine and perspiration. It has other virtues besides these and is very useful, as the physicians tell us. But this concerns something that we are not allowed to make (from the religious viewpoint), which makes talking of it superfluous and unnecessary, and therefore we will not mention the various kinds and how they could be used in the upkeep of health. . . .

The benefits of wine are many if it is taken in the proper amount, as it keeps the body in a healthy condition and cures many illnesses. But the knowledge of its consumption is hidden from the masses. What they want is to get drunk and inebriety causes harm. The one who taught that intemperance is useful once a month is in error, because it causes only injury and abrogates the strength of the entire body, particularly of the brain. The small amount that is useful must be taken after the food leaves the stomach. Young children should not come close to it because it hurts them and causes harm to their body and soul. Galen has already said: A child should abstain from it till the age of twenty-one. The older a man is, the more beneficial the wine is for him. Old people need it most.[14]

Modern authors have commented pertinently on the medicinal use of wine by the Moslems. Laufer states that the Arabians and Persians, "though they are forbidden wine by the Koran, bestow much pains on the cultivation of the grape, and suppose that the different kinds possess distinguishing medicinal qualities."[15] Some aspects of medieval Moslem culture are reflected in the *Arabian Nights*, fanciful tales centered about life in Baghdad during the reign of Caliph Haroun-al-Rashid (A.D. 766-809). A patron of learning, this famous caliph encouraged the translation and copying into Arabic of the works of Hippocrates, Galen, Dioscorides, and other great Greek classicists. Although the text of the *Arabian Nights* as we know it apparently was not assembled until the fourteenth century, it is believed to have been arabicized from ninth-century Persian sources. A portion relates to diagnosis of disease and to other aspects of Arabic medicine, including this widely-quoted passage concerning wine:

As for the advantages that be therein, it [wine] disperseth stone and gravel from the kidneys and strengtheneth the viscera and banisheth care, and moveth to generosity and preserveth health and digestion; it conserveth the body, expelleth disease from the joints, purifieth the frame of corrupt humours, engendereth cheerfulness, gladdeneth the heart of man and keepeth up the natural heat; it contracteth the bladder, enforceth the liver and removeth obstructions, reddeneth the cheeks, cleareth away maggots from the brain and defferreth grey hairs. In short, had not Allah (to whom be honour and glory!) forbidden it, there were not on the face of the earth aught fit to stand in its stead.[16]

Actually, the Koranic prohibition of wine has seldom interfered with its medicinal use in Moslem countries, because Islamic law has long been interpreted to permit the use of wine as medicine. That the conflict is more apparent than real is made clear by Dr. Mahmoud F. Hoballah, director of the Islamic Center at Washington, D. C., who writes:[17]

It is a well-known fact, accepted by all Muslim schools of thought, that when any food or drink has become necessary for a man because his health, his life or the duration of his life is dependent upon it, this kind of food or drink cannot be prohibited; necessity makes it lawful for the use of Muslims. The proofs to be cited for such a statement are many, from which the following Quranic verses are mentioned:

"Whoever is driven by necessity, with no inclination to transgression, God is indeed often forgiving, most merciful." —Chapter 5, part of Verse 4.

"Whoever is forced by necessity, without wilful disobedience, nor transgressing due limits,—thy Lord is often forgiving, most merciful."—Chapter 6, Verse 145.

The major Arabic contributions to the healing arts were in pharmacy. The basic elements of Greek, Syriac, Arabic, and Hindu materia medica were combined in the *Book of the Foundations of the True Properties of the Remedies*, an exhaustive treatise by the tenth-century Persian pharmacologist, Mansur the Great (Abū Mansūr Muwaffak ibn 'Alī al-Harawī). Mansur wrote of various preparations with wine, advising, for example, that if one gargled or washed the mouth with "wine in which [plum] leaves have been boiled, he alleviates all complaints of catarrh which exist in the throat, neck and chest."[18]

The Arabic writers emphasized syrups and juleps,[19] devised hundreds of new medicaments, discovered sulphuric acid, and may have been the first to distill alcohol.[20] In addition, they organized the loose ends of pharmacy, separated the arts of the apothecary and alchemist from those of the physician, and established at Baghdad in 754 A.D. the first apothecary shop. But the principal service of the Arabic physicians was in realizing the contributions to medicine by the great Greeks, organizing them into coherent texts, and reintroducing them into Western Europe via Spain after the Moslem conquests.

BIBLIOGRAPHY

1. *Syrian Anatomy, Pathology and Therapeutics.* Trans., E. A. Wallis Budge, London, Oxford University Press, 1913, 2 vols.
2. Lutz, H. F.: *Viticulture and Brewing in the Ancient Orient, op. cit.*, p. 35. Lutz also states (p. 37) that ancient Arabia imported most of its wine from Syria.
3. Surah XVI: 67, 69.
4. Robinson, James Harvey: *The Ordeal of Civilization.* New York, Harper & Brothers, 1926, p. 75.
5. Walsh: *Old-Time Makers of Medicine, op. cit.*, p. 117.
6. Sobhy Bey, George P.: *Lectures in the History of Medicine.* Cairo, Fouad I University Press, 1949, p. 63.
7. Gruner, O. Cameron: *A Treatise on the Canon of Medicine of Avicenna.* London, Luzac & Co., 1930, pp. 409-410.
8. *Ibid.:* p. 411.
9. *Ibid.:* pp. 379-380, 412.
10. *Ibid.:* pp. 434-435, 412.
11. *Ibid.:* p. 411.
12. Sobhy Bey: *op. cit.*, p. 63.
13. Gruner: *op. cit.*, p. 412, Rule 809.

14. Moses ben Maimon: *The Preservation of Youth, Essays on Health*. Trans. from the original Arabic and introduction by H. L. Gordon, New York, Philosophical Library, 1958, pp. 32, 81-82.

15. Laufer, Berthold: *Sino-Iranica*. Chicago, Field Museum of Natural History Publication 201, Vol. XV, No. 3, 1919, p. 241.

16. *The Book of the Thousand Nights and a Night*. The Richard F. Burton Club, 1897, Vol. V, p. 224. The 452nd night, "Abu al-Husn and his Slave Girl Tawaddud."

17. Personal communication.

18. Reed, Howard S.: *A Short History of the Plant Sciences*. Waltham, Mass., Chronica Botanica Co., 1942, p. 53.

19. From the Persian *gulab*, the Arabic *julāb*.

20. The name of alcohol is believed to have been derived from the Arabic *al koh'l*, literally "the stain," referring to the fine powder of antimony used by the women of the East for painting the eyebrows. Presumably because of the fineness of the powder, the name was later applied to rectified spirits, a significance unknown in Arabia.

8

Monastic Medicine and the Galenicals

DURING THE EARLY CENTURIES of the Dark Ages that followed the collapse of Rome, the Church became the center of healing in Western Europe. In this troublous era of wars and famines, medicine became a part of church dogma, and "faith" was its first principle. Experimentation was suppressed. The clerical healers believed in the miracles and curative powers of saints and holy relics. They identified various saints with parts of the body and named diseases for them, such as St. Anthony's fire for erysipelas and St. Vitus's dance for the spasmodic twitchings characteristic of chorea. Their credulity, burdened with piety, popularized wonder cures, and sometimes, when the cure failed, the healer was put to death.

The monasteries encompassed the hospitals and the pharmacies, and were the repositories for the surviving manuscripts of ancient civilization. Close by them were hostelries where the traveling physicians, who brought from Alexandria and Spain the arts of Greek and Arabic medicine, could lodge. The eclectic monks chose not to practice surgery. Their principal medicaments were mixtures of plant substances compounded in wine according to the recipes of Galen. The active principles of these plant substances became known in subsequent centuries as the galenicals.

Each monastery had its vineyard, since wine was indispensable for religious purposes, and there is ample evidence of its widespread dietary use by clergy and laity. Spiced (mulled) wines, similar to the medicinal wines, were also used festively, and these had added significance in symbolizing oaths and pledges of fealty. It was a time when nobles swore friendship on cups of spiced wine—and cut the throats of their drinking partners.

The studious monks translated into Latin the Greek manuscripts of Hippocrates, Pliny, Dioscorides, Galen, and the Byzantine physicians, and also many manuscripts that were spurious. The methods of Hippocrates were censored and his observations misquoted while the dogmatic teachings of Galen were accepted without question. The only real service to medical science by the monks during the Dark Ages was the preservation of those ancient manuscripts that came into their possession.

During the famines and epidemics of the sixth century, the Church, having gradually assumed the functions of government and education, was also called upon to assist in the relief of sickness and distress. The monasteries became the centers of mercy for the people of their respective communities. The monks established hospitals to care for the sick and, in addition to their spiritual ministrations, supplied as much orthodox medicine as they could command. Prayers were uttered while medicines were administered, and the saints were invoked for their aid in healing. Considering the monastic neglect of surgery, it is not surprising to find Bishop Gregory of Tours (d. 594), in his *History of the Franks*, extolling the endurance of pain as one of the highest of human virtues.[1]

The Galenic recipes for medicinal wines were in use throughout Western Europe. Many remedies of the Greek and Roman physicians are found in medieval Anglo-Saxon medicine, early remnants of which have survived in *The Leechbook of Bald*. This oldest extant treatise of leechcraft is believed to have been written in the early part of the tenth century, before the Normans invaded England. In the *Leechbook*, together with the charms and spells of folk medicine, are found these typical treatments:

For ana worm [apparently an infection of the skin]: Rub down into ale or wine seeds of radish and of colewort, let the man drink it long and often till he be bettered.

For a broken limb: Take vinegar and sour crumbs of barley loaf and earthworms, mingle together and bind on; wet the joint with vinegar or sour ale.[2]

Evidently the Anglo-Saxon leeches, lacking supplies of the specific wines named in the recipes of the ancients, substituted the common beverage of Britain, ale.

The books of hygienic regimen were a product of the

monasteries, and in these the dietetic and medicinal uses of wine, both natural and altered, were endorsed. The hospitals of the monasteries laid the foundation for the eventual development of the medical schools, of which Salerno, in southern Italy, was one of the first.

Founded on the site of a ninth-century Benedictine hospital, the School of Salerno drew a faculty of both clerical and lay practitioners, who taught an organized art of healing that eventually spread throughout Europe. The use of wine was an integral part of Salernitan medicine. It was prescribed as a nutrient, as an internal antiseptic, and as a restorative; and it was the universal menstruum for other medicinal substances. It is the one therapeutic agent mentioned most frequently in the code of health of Salerno, the *Regimen sanitatis salernitanum*.[3] This eleventh-century poem, which epitomizes the medical literature of the time, is primarily a set of regulations for the preservation of health, emphasizing diet and blood-letting and containing common recipes for the medicaments classed as simples. It was committed to memory by thousands of medieval physicians, who regarded it as they did the sacred Scriptures.

The *Regimen* has appeared in nearly three hundred editions, addressed in various languages to various European rulers. Packard[4] has contended that the original text was that addressed to "England's King," whom he identifies as Robert, Duke of Normandy, who claimed but never won the English crown. Robert, the rebellious eldest son of William the Conqueror, was treated at Salerno in 1099 for a fistulous wound which he had received at Jerusalem during the First Crusade. The English translation of the *Regimen* by Sir John Haryngton, first published in 1607, begins with this verse of proverbial wisdom:

> The *Salerno Schoole* doth by these lines impart
> All health to *Englands King*, and doth aduise
> From care his head to keepe, from wrath his heart,
> Drinke not much wine, sup light, and soone arise,
> When meate is gone, long sitting breedeth smart:
> And after-noone still waking keepe your eyes.
> When mou'd you find your selfe to *Natures Needs*,
> Forbeare them not, for that much danger breeds,
> Use three Physicions still; first Doctor *Quiet*,
> Next Doctor *Merry-man*, and Doctor *Dyet*.[5]

It continues with the following advice for selecting wines:

> Chuse wine you meane shall serue you all the yeere,
> Well-sauor'd tasting well, and coloured cleere.
> Fiue qualities there are, wines praise advancing,
> *Strong, Beautifull*, and *Fragrant, coole* and *dancing*.[6]

The *Regimen* advises that wine be drunk when eating meat, especially pork:

> *Porke* without wine is not so good to eate,
> As *sheepe* with wine, it medicine is and meat,
> Tho Intrailes of a beast be not the best,
> Yet are some intrailes better than the rest.[7]

It describes the effects, physiologic and socio-emotional, of different wines:

> *Red wine* doth make the voyce oft-time to seeke,
> And hath a binding qualitie to that;
> *Canarie*, and *Madera*, both are like
> To make one leane indeed: (but wot you what)

> Who say they make one leane, would make one laffe
> They meane, they make one leane upon a staffe.
> *Wine, women, Baths,* by Art or Nature warme,
> Us'd or abus'd do men much good or harme.[8]

It selects wine of Gascony for special consideration:

> Egges newly laid, are nutritiue to eate,
> And rosted Reare [rare] are easie to digest.
> Fresh *Gascoigne* wine is good to drinke with meat,
> *Broth* strengthens nature aboue all the rest. . . .
> Remember eating new laid Egges and soft,
> For euery Egge you eate you drinke as oft.[9]

It extols the virtues of bread and wine:

> Four speciall vertues hath a sop in wine,
> It maketh the teeth white, it cleares the eyne,
> It addes unto an emptie stomack fulnesse,
> And from a stomack fill'd it takes the dulnesse.[10]

It cites typical prescriptions for medicated and condi-
mented wines:

> If in your drinke you mingle *Rew* with *Sage,*
> All poyson is expeld by power of those,
> And if you would withall Lusts heat asswage,
> Adde to them two the gentle flowre of Rose:
> Would not be sea-sicke when seas do rage,
> *Sage-water* drink with wine before he goes.
> *Salt, Garlicke, Parsly, Pepper, Sage, and Wine,*
> Make sawces for all meates both course and fine.
> Of washing of your hands much good doth rise,
> Tis wholesome, cleanely, and relieues your eyes.[11]

And the *Regimen* advises and prescribes, according to the
season, bathing, sweating, diet, and "Venus recreation":

> The spring is moist, of temper good and warme,

> Then best it is to bathe, to sweate, and purge,
> Then may one ope a veine in either arme,
> If boyling bloud or feare of agues urge:
> Then *Venus* recreation doth no harme,
> Yet may too much thereof turne to a scourge.
> In Summers heat (when choller hath dominion)
> Coole meates and moist are best in some opinion:
> The *Fall* is like the *Spring*, but endeth colder,
> With Wines and Spice the Winter may be bolder.[12]

The School of Salerno was open to women students, the most famous of whom was Trotula, a clinician of the eleventh century, who sometimes is referred to as Madame Trot or Mother Trot of Salerno. Trotula is credited with books on obstetrics, cosmetic hygiene, and related subjects, in which she describes many uses of wine. She treated prolapse of the uterus after childbirth by applying "hot wine in which butter has been boiled."[13] In a chapter dealing with the care of infants, Trotula re-emphasizes a famous remedy:

We help a disease of children which is a very severe cough by taking hyssop and wild thyme cooked in wine and giving it to them to drink, or we mix grains of juniper with wine for a drink.[14]

The recipe for an ointment to be used for burned or chapped areas makes artful use of the anesthetic principles of aromatic ethers:

Take an apple, Armenian *clod*, mastic, *olibanum*, hot wine, wax and *sepum* . . . mix these together . . . then we strain through a cloth. It should be directed that after one has been anointed with this ointment, the burned area should be covered with a leaf of ivy cooked in vinegar or wine. . . . This is a good remedy![15]

For foulness of breath during pregnancy:

> . . . owing to a fault of the stomach, let tops of myrtle be grated and cooked in wine until reduced to one half. Let this wine be drunk on an empty stomach.[16]

During the eleventh century, many Arabic medical manuscripts were brought to Salerno by Constantine the African (*ca.* 1020-1087). These are believed to have been the source of one of the most important Salernitan compilations of medical recipes, the *Antidotarium Nicolai*, which catalogued one hundred and fifty galenicals. Its author, Nicholas Praepositus, was director of the school. A manuscript copy of this *antidotarium* written in the thirteenth century begins to show the elements of systematized pharmacy. A fourteenth-century copy included prescriptions for various diseases, a short treatise on wines, formulas for oil of roses and oil of mandragora, and three recipes for making *Hiera Picra* (Holy Bitter), one of the three great historic remedies used by the Greek physicians in the temples of Asklēpios. In this fashion Constantinus Africanus and Nicholas of Salerno bridged the gap between Arabic medicine and that of the late Middle Ages.

During this period the functions of the apothecary quite naturally fell to the monks. Nearly every monastery in Europe had its "cupboard" of medicinal agents, the forerunner of the modern pharmacy. The cupboards in which the drugs and spices were stored were known as the *armaria pigmentaria*. The apothecary or *pigmentarius*, who was monitor of the cupboard, dispensed the medicines to the sick and wounded, subject to supervision by the monk-physician. With the increase in the number of remedies and the greater demand for them, the *armarium pigmentarium* eventually became the monastic pharmacy.

In the beginning the medicinal plants were gathered in their natural state from the woods and fields neighboring the monasteries. Later in their gardens, the *herbularia*, the monks cultivated the plants which were to be used as medicaments. In the latter part of the eighth and the beginning of the ninth century, great emphasis was placed upon the cultivation of special medicinal plants. Among those grown in the *herbularia* were rosemary, rue, sage, marshmallow, savine, fever-few, and peppermint. In a capitulary of a thirteenth-century monastery, one encounters in addition aniseed, caraway, cumin, coriander, fennel, laurel, and mustard.

The belief that diseases were caused by miasms or bad odors brought spices into use as safeguards against illness. For centuries, and even in recent years, cubes of camphor or bags of foul-smelling asafoetida have been hung around the necks of children [a recollection of the author's own childhood] in order to ward off illness during wintertime and especially during epidemics. As a result of this superstition, spices came into prominence during the Middle Ages as drugs rather than as culinary products.[17] The wines to which they were added were the theriacs of ancient and medieval times and the forerunners of modern vermouths, bitters, apéritifs, liqueurs, and cordials.

Modern research has confirmed the values of the essential (volatile) oils contained in the various herbs and spices, values known empirically to the ancient and medieval healers who used them as carminatives and as internal antiseptics through the many centuries.

Cordials (from the Latin *cor:* heart) originated as medicinal preparations in the monastic practice of alchemy, the search for the universal remedy, the elixir of immortality. The monastic philosophers and alchemists, believing that base metals were diseased relatives of the only perfect one—gold—applied this concept to the diseases of human beings, and sought to transmute other metals into gold. They conceived of the elixir as a "potable gold." One of the cordials originally compounded in the monasteries and still popular in the present century is *Goldwasser*, in which flakes of gold are suspended.

In some monasteries a room adjoining the *armarium pigmentarium* was equipped with copper alembics. Here distillation was practiced, first of aromatic and cordial *aquas*, and eventually of wine to produce *aqua ardens*, alcohol in the form of brandy. Although distillation had been practiced earlier in Arabia, it was the monks of the thirteenth century who introduced the art into Europe.

Wootton, in *Chronicles of Pharmacy*, has attributed to the *Book of Fires*, written by Marcus Graecus about 1300, the first definite recipe for distilling wine:

Take a black wine, thick and old. To ¼ lb. of this add 2 scruples of sulphur vivum in very fine powder, and 2 scruples of common salt in coarse fragments, and 1 or 2 lbs. of tartar extracted from a good white wine. Place all in a copper alembic and distill off the aqua ardens.[18]

The newly prepared spirit of wine was extolled in extravagant phrases, and as a sovereign remedy for human ills it took its place at the head of the medicaments. The spirit of wine was the elixir of life, and to designate it as *aqua vitae* was a natural consequence. At the same time, brandy took its place with wine as a menstruum for the cordials and other medicaments, long before the distillates of grain and sugar came into use for these purposes.

The medical schools of the time, although their faculties included clergymen, were not monastic institutions. After Salerno, rival schools were established at Naples, Palermo, Montpellier, and Bologna, and at all of these the independent study of medicine was encouraged and wine was used therapeutically. The founder of the Medical School of Bologna was Thaddeus of Florence (1223-1303), who compiled a therapeutic text modestly called *De virtute aquae vitae, quae etiam dicitur aqua ardens* (On the virtues of the water of life, which is also called fiery water). Thaddeus was called "the great doctor" by Dante in the *Commedia*.[19]

During the entire monastic period, however, except for the distillation of brandy and the manufacture of cordials as phases of alchemy and pharmacy, few advances were made in human knowledge. Through these centuries the monasteries and medical schools merely preserved remnants of Greek and Arabic medicine. It was through these remnants that the ancient lore of the medicinal uses of wine was safeguarded.

BIBLIOGRAPHY

1. Gregory, Bishop of Tours: *The History of the Franks*. Trans., O. M. Dalton, Oxford, Clarendon Press, 1927, Vol. II, pp. 418-423.

2. Payne, Joseph F.: *English Medicine in the Anglo-Saxon Times.* Oxford, The Clarendon Press, 1904, pp. 46, 85.

3. *Regimen sanitatis salernitanum;* The School of Salernum. English version by Sir John Haryngton, with introduction by Francis R. Packard. New York, Paul B. Hoeber, 1920.

4. *Ibid.:* pp. 25-29.

5. *Ibid.:* p. 75.

6. *Ibid.:* p. 82.

7. *Ibid.:* p. 92.

8. *Ibid.:* p. 84.

9. *Ibid.:* p. 81.

10. *Ibid.:* p. 108.

11. *Ibid.:* p. 91.

12. *Ibid.:* p. 130.

13. Trotula: *The Diseases of Women.* Trans., Elizabeth Mason-Hohl, The Ward Ritchie Press, 1940, p. 28.

14. *Ibid.:* p. 34.

15. *Ibid.:* p. 29.

16. *Ibid.:* p. 44.

17. The unsanitary conditions prevailing during the Middle Ages brought a demand for aromatic substances which could cover bad odors, disinfect spoiled foods, and preserve those not yet spoiled. Because foods thus treated were believed to be less capable of producing disease, the spices became invested with curative virtues. In the ancient Orient, the manufacturer of spiced wines was at the same time a perfumer.

18. Wootton, A. C.: *Chronicles of Pharmacy.* London, Macmillan and Co., Ltd., 1910, Vol. I, pp. 328-329.

19. Canto XII.

Arnald the Catalan

ELEVEN CENTURIES AFTER GALEN, the Greek physician who first scientifically catalogued medicinal wines, Arnald of Villanova (*ca.* 1235-1311) wrote the *Liber de vinis*, which established the use of wine as a recognized system of therapy during the late Middle Ages. With the prestige of its famous author, this book was copied in many manuscripts and translated into many languages. After the introduction of printing in 1438, it appeared in at least twenty-one printed editions and guided practitioners throughout Western Europe in the specific treatment of many diseases with wines.

Physician to popes, kings, and paupers, prolific author and noted teacher, Arnald epitomized the past of medicine and set the stage for its future when, following the crusades, medieval healing entered a period of temporary enlightenment. Among his numerous medical treatises were the *Breviary of Practice*, a complete manual for physicians; the *Parables*, a set of 345 pithy aphorisms about health; and a famous commentary on the *Regimen sanitatis* of Salerno. None was more influential than his book on wine.

Arnald was born near Valencia into a humble Catalonian family, and grew up in poverty. His early education was acquired in a Dominican school for boys, where he learned languages, philosophy, and the natural sciences, and prepared for the study of medicine. Details of his early career are lacking, but he probably received his medical training in Naples, and also in Valencia, where he was associated with prominent Arabian physicians. Joining the faculty of the medical school of Montpellier, he became its most distinguished instructor. In 1285 he was called to Villafranca to treat King Peter III of Aragon. Later he treated Pope Boniface VIII for the stone and became physician in ordinary to the pontiff. He also served Popes Benedict XI and Clement V, and is said to have cured Pope Innocent V of the plague with his prescription of gold quenched in wine.

A brilliant and original thinker, Arnald contributed independent observations about medicine and also about political issues and theology. The latter got him into difficulties; his unorthodox theological treatises caused him to be accused of heresy. He was arrested under the Inquisition, was tried and convicted at Paris in 1299, and was saved by Pope Boniface, who approved of the conviction but, valuing Arnald's medical treatment, did not condemn his theology. Although he escaped the Inquisition physically, Arnald was anathematized after his death, and his religious and philosophical writings were burned.

Arnald valued wines, both natural and medicated, above drugs alone. In the *Parables* he emphasized that "the modest and wise physician will never hasten to drugs unless compelled by necessity."[1] He used wines as restoratives, as antiseptics, and in the preparation of poultices. He made significant contributions in the rational treatment of wounds, a subject which will be discussed in the next chapter. But throughout his writings, Arnald's genius as a physician is beclouded by his reverence for the ancient authorities and for their doctrine of the Humors—coldness, heat, dryness, and moisture. The *Liber de vinis* is thus an admixture of his independent observations with the medical folklore of antiquity. An example is the following passage in praise of wine for body and soul:

Now the time has come to prepare the wines that are used for medicinal purposes, and particularly the white wine that suits the human body best. For it is more subtile and more receptive to all the vapors of everything pressed into it. It carries the virtues of incorporated substances through all members, with delectation and in a natural way. This is why its virtues are highly praised by experienced philosophers and physicians, for wine has in itself great quality in the order of human nature. Ruffus [Rufus of Ephesus, 98-117 A.D.], indeed, says speaking about it: Wine not only strengthens the natural heat but also clarifies turbid blood and opens the passages of the whole body. It strengthens also the members. And its goodness is not only revealed in the body but also in the soul, for it makes the soul merry and lets it forget sadness. . . .[2]

Arnald wrote his work on wine about 1310, at the height of his career, as a purely medical treatise. The German version, printed at Nürnberg in 1478, is dedicated to "the King of France," but Sigerist states that the original dedication was to Robert of Anjou, King of Naples. The *Liber de vinis* recommends the use of wine for all ages:

If wine is taken in right measure it suits every age, every time and every region. It is becoming to the old because it opposes their dryness. To the young it is a food, because the nature of wine is the same as that of young people. But to children it is also a food because it increases their natural heat. It is a medicine to them because it dries out the moisture they have drawn from their mother's body. No physician blames the use of wine by healthy people unless he blames the quantity or the admixture of water. . . . Hence it comes that men experienced in the art of healing have chosen the wine and have written many chapters about it and have declared it to be a useful embodiment or combination of all things for common usage. It truly is most friendly to human nature.[3]

Arnald apparently observed that wine was valuable in preventing ailments caused by polluted water, since he directed that any water added should be mixed well in advance of drinking:

Watered wine is very wholesome. I knew a physician of great repute who drank no other wine. There also is no better wine for sick people. For wine and water mix well. . . . The water, however, must come from a good fresh fountain, and the wine must be mixed before it is brought to the table. It happens that many gentlemen and prelates have the water poured into the wine at the moment when they want to drink. This leads to disturbance, flatulence and indigestion of the stomach. . . .[4]

He attributed special virtues to raisin wine, to which he added cinnamon:

It is a wine that is proper for sick old people, also for melancholics and phlegmatics, and it particularly makes women fat. It eases the chest, strengthens the stomach, adds substance to the liver and strengthens it. It warms the blood, opposes putrefaction, and removes nausea and mucosity of the stomach. It is also useful for coughing and asthma, and it naturally loosens the hardened bowels and astringes the loose bowels, such as in dysentery and similar conditions. It has the faculty of strengthening the retentive and expulsive function. It is good for short breath and for the cardiac disease . . . When it is used, ulcers cannot develop in the body. And whoever uses it steadily will never have any disease from evil humours, so God will.[5]

To heal "the insane and the demented who have to be bound," and to restore their reason, Arnald prescribed wine of oxtongue (an herb of the chicory family), and testified to having witnessed a spectacular cure:

Its roots shall be well cleaned and shall be macerated in wine until the wine has taken the taste and potence of the roots. This wine shall be drunk steadily for it drives out the melancholic, choleric and burnt humours through the urine. It restores the brain that has been poisoned by the vapor of melancholy. . . . I can testify this on my conscience because I saw a woman, born in the city of Paris, who very frequently was deprived of her senses by some anger and melancholy and became garrulous and was using loose talk so that she had to be bound in her home until her wrath had gone. She was given the above-mentioned remedy by a pilgrim who came to her house asking for charity, and thus she was cured.[6]

Wine strained through ground winter cherries was Arnald's extraordinary remedy for urinary troubles. He used it to relieve a bloated cardinal, perhaps by virtue of the mildly anesthetic benzaldehyde contained in the cherries:

It drives the urine immediately, whatever the retention may have been, and extracts the sandy matter from the kidneys and bladder in great quantities and so apparently that you could collect it with the hand. And this wine when used frequently, remedies such pains. There was a cardinal in my time who had not passed any urine for three days and was swollen and bloated. No other remedy would help him. Then upon the advice of an unknown doctor he drank this wine and discharged urine in great quantities. So the good sir was cured.[7]

To beautify women and to give them that awe-inspiring "white, subtle and pleasant complexion," and, incidentally, to cure paralysis, the *Liber de vinis* directs:

Put ginger and cinnamon bark into wine and distill it like rose-water. It is also good for all cold complexions and ailments and particularly for paralysis which is an ailment of the limbs.[8]

Arnald prescribed a preparation of "rosemary wine" as a dentrifrice to strengthen the gums, and as a hairwash to prevent and cure baldness. He wrote that "cancer washed frequently with it is cured," a belief that survives among some groups even today. He claimed that his recipe of "wine in which gold has been quenched" would strengthen and ennoble the heart, clarify the spirit, purify the blood, preserve youth, and make people persevere in their work. He described a wine infused with eyebright [*euphrasia*] as a remedy for all defects of vision, and incidentally furnished evidence of the early medieval use of eye-glasses:

... when this wine is used it undoubtedly has no equal in the treatment of the eyes. This has been testified by reliable people who have tried it on themselves. For while they were unable to see without eye-glasses before, they were able to read small letters without glasses after its use.

Altogether, some forty-nine medicinal wines are offered in various manuscripts of Arnald's book as specifics for scores of diseases, including malaria, tuberculosis, gout, jaundice, epilepsy, pleurisy, intestinal parasites, scabies, seasickness, sterility, and loss of memory.[9] Furnishing physicians with a complete and convenient set of directions for the treatment of virtually all the physical and mental ills of mankind, the *Liber de vinis* readily became a "best-seller" among the medical books of the fifteenth and sixteenth centuries.

Wootton states that Arnald was also the first to make specific reference to the spirit of wine—brandy, which apparently had not long been known. Arnald called it "aqua vini" [water of wine], and added, "but some name it ... aqua vitae [water of life] or water which preserves itself always, and golden water. It is well called water of life . . . because it strengthens the body and prolongs life."[10] He also wrote that "fresh wounds washed with the spirit of wine attain the desired healing faster than any other."[11] In thus noting that the distillate of wine inhibits infection, he probably was the first physician in history to record the use of a concentrated alcoholic solution as an antiseptic for wounds.

However, his interest in brandy apparently was not primarily for its therapeutic values, but in connection with his practice of alchemy. Arnald was closely associated in the search for a universal elixir of life with the noted Majorcan alchemist Raymond Lully. The alchemists were not the rabble, but the most highly educated men in the community. Roger Bacon, Albertus Magnus, and to a lesser degree the famous theologian Thomas Aquinas were all believers in the philosophers' stone. In Germany, for three centuries after Arnald men of this stamp continued to cherish a belief in this form of magic. Even Martin Luther did not hesitate to express his approval of the black art.

Among the numerous writings of Arnald were the treatise on *The Preservation of Youth and the Retardation of Age*, in which he expressed his belief that "out of wine ... [and the bodies of metals] may be made a water of life."[12] Another was the book on *Poisons*, which contains his often-quoted statement that

In this book I propose, with God's help, to consider diseases of women, since women are poisonous creatures. I shall then treat of the bites of venomous beasts.[13]

He is said to have written altogether one hundred and twenty-three books and treatises. Most of them were destroyed by the Inquisition after Arnald was drowned in the Mediterranean in 1311 while on one of his political missions.

Noted historians of medicine have described Arnald of

Villanova as one of the most colorful figures of the Middle Ages, as one of the first men of his time to pursue independent medical investigations, as the inventor of modern tinctures in which the virtues of herbs are extracted by alcohol, and as a pioneer in the classification of diseases. Yet it would seem that one of his key roles in the history of medicine was in indoctrinating and guiding many successive generations of European physicians in the therapeutic uses of wine.

BIBLIOGRAPHY

1. Arnald von Villanova: *Parabeln der Heilkunst.* Trans., Paul Diepgen, from the Latin. Leipzig, J. H. Barth, 1922, pp. 13, 50-61.
2. *Arnald of Villanova's Book on Wine.* Trans., Henry E. Sigerist, from the German version of Wilhelm von Hirnkofen. New York, Schuman's, 1943, p. 24. Sigerist questions the authorship of these passages and suggests that Hirnkofen may have taken them from an anonymous Latin manuscript.
3. *Ibid.:* pp. 24-25.
4. *Ibid.:* pp. 42-43.
5. *Ibid.:* pp. 34-35.
6. *Ibid.:* p. 34.
7. *Ibid.:* p. 40.
8. *Ibid.:* p. 41.
9. *Ibid.:* pp. 35-37. The Hirnkofen edition is abbreviated, containing only 25 of the medicated wines.
10. Wootton: *Chronicles of Pharmacy, op. cit.,* Vol. I, p. 329.
11. *The Parables, op. cit.,* p. 53.
12. Emerson, E. R.: *Beverages Past and Present.* New York, G. P. Putnam's Sons, 1908, Vol. I, p. 555.
13. Guthrie, D.: *A History of Medicine.* London, Thomas Nelson and Sons, Ltd., 1945, p. 113.

10

Surgeons and Barber-Surgeons

T HE HISTORY OF SURGERY, from the time of Hippocrates until the surgeon ceased to be classified with the barber, contains innumerable allusions to wine. As a drink to restore the wounded, its use antedates the Trojan Wars. Wine applied directly to wounds was, for more than two thousand years, the only antiseptic successful in preventing infection without injury to tissue. For this use, wine was not wholly replaced until late in the nineteenth century, when Lord Lister introduced antisepsis into surgery by subjecting both atmosphere and instruments to the cleansing effect of carbolic acid.

But the antiseptic treatment of wounds with wine was by no means universal. Before Lister, the prevailing dogma, attributed to Hippocrates and Galen, was that wounds healed best by "second intention," which involved inserting needles, setons, and irritant substances under the skin to provoke the generation of "laudable pus." The victims either got well in spite of such treatment or died in torment from infection. This was the fate of the uncounted thousands who were sacrificed in the continuous civil wars and crusades, and whose festering corpses littered the battlefields and byways during the Middle Ages. The belief in the value of suppuration undoubtedly caused more agonies and deaths among the wounded than any other superstition.

Actually, Hippocrates had described healing both by "first intention," the union of tissues without suppuration, and by "second intention"; and his rule was that "no wounds should be moistened with anything except wine unless the wound is in a joint." Galen, too, held this view, and recorded that the wounds of the Roman gladiators, when he applied to them dressings saturated in red wine, did not putrefy.[1] Nevertheless, the doctrine of "laudable pus" was imputed primarily to Galen, apparently through faulty translations by the Arabian commentators. On the pseudo-authority of the venerated Galen, the barbarous practice of promoting pus in wounds persisted in Europe until only a century ago.

During the Middle Ages there was a separation of surgery from medicine. The Moslems considered that to touch the body with the hands was unclean and unholy, while the early monastic healers depended mainly on galenic ointments and spiritual ministrations. Surgery was thus not only neglected, but at one time (in 1162) its practice by monks was prohibited by an edict of the Council of Tours, with the epithet *Ecclesia abhorret a sanguine*.

At the School of Salerno, healing by "second intention" was the accepted dogma of surgery; and the *Practica Chirurgiae*, written about 1170 by the leading surgeon of the school, Roger of Palermo, states definitely that pus should be generated in wounds.[2] Wine was an integral part of Salernitan medicine, but principally for internal use, although there is also the evidence that Trotula applied wine and vinegar to burned or chapped skin.[3]

The first surgeon of the Middle Ages to break with the practice of suppuration was Hugh of Lucca (Ugo Borgognoni), the city physician of Bologna, who during the Fifth Crusade treated Christian casualties at the siege of Damietta. While he left no record of his work, his disciple, Theodoric, wrote that Hugh effected the perfect healing of wounds with wine only, and without resort to ointments.[4]

In 1252, Bruno da Longoburgo, of the University of Padua, completed the *Chirurgia magna*, in which he emphasized the interdependence of surgery and medicine, and advocated rational wound antisepsis with wine. He noted that putrefaction is greater in summer than in winter, and recommended that in penetrating wounds of the abdominal cavity, if there were difficulty in bringing about the reposition of the intestines, these should first be pressed back with a sponge soaked in warm wine.[5]

It was Theodoric, the disciple and apparently the son of Hugh of Lucca, who first challenged the doctrine of "laudable pus." Theodoric (Teodorico Borgognoni,

1205-1296), upon completing his medical studies at the age of twenty-three, joined the newly-established Dominican Order, and became Bishop of Cervia, where in 1266 he wrote his textbook of surgery, the *Cyrurgia*, in which he denounced suppuration, declaring:

... for it is not necessary, as Roger and Roland [master and pupil] have written, as many of their disciples teach, and as all modern surgeons profess, that pus should be generated in wounds. No error can be greater than this. Such a practice is indeed to hinder nature, to prolong the disease, and to prevent the conglutination and consolidation of the wound.[6]

Theodoric rejected oils and salves as too slippery to effect union of the tissues; poultices as too moist to enhance healing; and powders as objectionable because they incarcerated decomposing matter. He insisted on wine as the best possible dressing for wounds.[7] Allbutt states that Theodoric, like Hugh,

... washed the wound with wine only, scrupulously removing every foreign particle; then they brought the edges together, forbidding any of the wine or other dressing to remain within. As with the genuine Hippocratic school, a dry and adhesive edge was their desire. Nature, they said, produces the means of union in a viscous exudation, or balm. ... In stale wounds they did their best to obtain union by cleansing, desiccation, and refreshing of the edges. Upon the outer surface they laid lint steeped in wine .... wine, after washing, purifying, and drying the raw surfaces, evaporates.[8]

The principles of Theodoric were upheld by one of the ablest Italian physicians and surgeons of the thirteenth century, William of Salicet. Salicet (Guglielmo Salicetti, *ca.* 1210-1277), a pupil of Bruno da Longoburgo, was professor at Bologna, city physician of Verona, and had acquired surgical experience both in hospitals and on the battlefield. He advocated union by "first intention," insisted on cleanliness as the most important factor in obtaining good surgical results, and when operating upon septic cases used strong wine as a dressing.[9]

Salicet's pupil, Lanfranc (Guido Lanfranchi), driven from Italy by the violent rulers of Milan, settled in Paris, where at the Collège de Saint Côme he espoused and practiced the teachings of Salicet and became the virtual founder of the French school of surgery. Lanfranc, though a brilliant contributor to surgical techniques, lapsed into the practice of suppuration. Meanwhile, his contemporary, Arnald of Villanova, practicing at Montpellier, having observed the antiseptic value of the spirit of wine, was championing tinctures made with it as superior aids in wound surgery.[10] Although alcohol attained considerable vogue in the treatment of wounds, its use was not as extensive as that of the milder and more gentle antiseptic, wine.

A valiant stand against suppuration was made by the famous thirteenth-century physician, surgeon and anatomist, Henri de Mondeville (1260-1320), the disciple of Lanfranc. Mondeville, a native of Normandy, lecturer at the University of Montpellier and physician to Philip the Fair, advocated simple cleanliness as taught by Hippocrates, contending in his surgical treatise that pus "is not a stage of healing but a complication"[11] and that "wounds dry much better before suppuration than after it." He advised that nothing whatever should be put into a wound, and used wine principally as a tonic or "wound drink" to strengthen his patients.[12]

Whatever Mondeville and his predecessors had accomplished toward the cause of rational asepsis was destroyed by the celebrated French army surgeon, Guy de Chauliac (1300-1368). Although de Chauliac used wine unstintingly in the treatment of wounds, and recommended rinsing the mouth with wine in order to prevent dental decay,[13] he also provoked suppuration. De Chauliac, a knowledgeful medical historian, aggressively assailed Theodoric as a plagiarist, and stoutly supported the pseudo-Galenic doctrine of surgical interference with natural healing. With his great prestige as a scholar and as physician to the Popes at Avignon, his reactionary views, expressed in the *Chirurgia magna*, retarded progress in surgery for more than five hundred years.[14]

In England, antiseptic surgery through the use of wine was practiced to some extent by that nation's earliest surgeon, John of Arderne (1307-1377), who served the nobility, the wealthy landowners, and the higher clergy, and was an army surgeon in the Hundred Years War. In his surgical writings, he taught that wounds should heal without suppuration, that local applications to them should be as little irritating as possible, and that the dressings should not be changed frequently.[15] Although well educated, Arderne showed the influence and mysticism of the early Saxon leeches, even including acceptance and use of the doctrine of charms. His employment of wine as a menstruum is illustrated by the following recipes, which reflect both old folk-medicine and an assiduous study of the contributions of the Arabian physicians:

Against Deafness: Eggs of ants and earthworms beaten up with white wine and distilled in an alembic and, after cleansing the body, injected into the ear makes the deaf hear and stops tinnitus. And if from a cold cause let the juice of a leek be added. . . . In hot causes, too, let absinthe be infused in water with mallow and applied; also in cold causes let a decoction be made with white wine.[16]

For pain due to an accident or a blow: The crumb of rye bread is useful moistened with warm wine and juice of absinthe and poultices. . . .[17]

Against Rupture: The four consolidating juices [Comfrey, Bugle, the daisy, and larkspur] and polybody [oakfern]. . . . Wash them with the best red wine that can be procured. Put them in a glass vessel and let them stand for 4 days. . . . And when you wish to operate give it to the patient to drink and place the lees over the rupture with a bandage applied secundum artum. Do this for nine days and the rupture will be cured.[18]

To break a stone: [Remove] a boar's bladder from its place and empty it of the water. Fill it with the blood of a he-goat aged four years or at any rate not less than three years old. The goat should have been fed on betony and saxifrage with fennel, parsley, butcher's broom, asparagus, milium solis and barley and afterwards in summer with ivy berries before the berries have begun to blacken. Give it to the patient to drink with lukewarm white wine. But if you wish to test it, put into the [pig's] bladder a similar stone . . . with the aforesaid blood and you will find the stone reduced to powder within seven days. . . .[19]

With the advent of firearms in the fourteenth and fifteenth centuries, battlefield surgery became horribly complicated by the nature of the abscesses produced by bird-dung nitrates and lead. Hieronymus Brunschwig (*ca.* 1450-1533), the Alsatian army surgeon who gave the first medical description of gunshot wounds, regarded them as poisoned, and maintained that the poison could be best removed by promoting suppuration with setons. In amputations, as was the custom, he applied boiling oil to the stump to check hemorrhage. Brunschwig made generous use of both wine and brandy as dressings and as wound drinks, and ascribed to them miraculous healing powers. He popularized *Aqua vite composita*, a mixture of strong Gascony wine, brandy, and herbs. He described this decoction, which resembled the modern cordials, as "wonderfull good, excellynge many other soveraygne oyles to dyvers dyseases." Of brandy, Brunschwig wrote, in *The Vertuose Boke of Distyllacyon:*

> It heleth also all stynkyng woundes when they be wasshed therwith . . . the canker in the mouthe . . . the rottyng tethe . . . in the lyppes, and in the tongue, when it is longe time holden in the mouthe . . . all scabbes of the body, and all colde swellyng, enoynted or wasshed therwith and also a lyttel thereof dronke. . . .[20]

A sixteenth-century opponent of suppuration was the noted Swiss physician and surgeon Paracelsus (Aureolus Theophrastus Bombastus von Hohenheim, 1493-1541), physician to the city of Basel and a pioneer of chemical pharmacology. Paracelsus denounced and publicly burned the works of Galen, revered Hippocrates, and taught that nature, the "natural balm," heals wounds.[21] Garrison mentions that Paracelsus popularized tinctures and alcoholic extracts, and describes him as "almost the only asepsist between Mondeville and Lister."[22]

Another great surgeon of the Middle Ages was Am-

broise Paré (1510-1590), a man who had the courage to
upset Renaissance thinking by abandoning the boiling oil,
the setons, and the lint that were customarily applied to
new gunshot wounds. One night in camp, when the
wounded were so numerous that his supply of oil gave
out, Paré was compelled to substitute a dressing, which
he compounded from the yolks of eggs, oil of roses, and
turpentine. That night he slept fitfully, fearing that in
the morning he would find the wounded whom he had
failed to cauterize, dead from septic poisoning. He was
rewarded to find them "feeling but little pain, their
wounds neither swollen nor inflamed," while the others
to whom he had applied the boiling oil were feverish,
their wounds swollen and painful. "Then," he afterwards
wrote, "I determined never again to burn thus so cruelly
the poor wounded by arquebuses."[23] Garrison comments
that had it not been for the fatty salves Paré continued to
apply "from some tenacity of superstition . . . he would
have been a true asepsist."[24]

Paré frequently dressed wounds with wine, brandy,
theriacs, and ointments compounded in wine; and as restoratives he used wine, vinegar, and ptisan (barley
water). In the *Apologie and Treatise*, he describes his
successful treatment of the Marquis d'Auret for an arque-
bus wound in the knee:

I made injections into the depth and cavities of the ulcers,
composed of aegyptiacum dissolved sometimes in brandy,
other times in wine. I applied . . . over them a large plaster of
diacalcitheos dissolved in wine. . . . Then I made him drinke
wine moderately tempered with water, knowing that it restores and quickens the vital forces.[25]

Paré was originally apprenticed (*ca.* 1532 or 1533) to a barber-surgeon of Paris. During the period when surgery was divorced from medicine, the humble barber-surgeons were allowed to perform such menial tasks as blood-letting, haircutting, shaving, and extracting teeth, and ultimately the talented did most of the actual surgery. During these times a caste system prevailed: the elite were the physicians, who prescribed drugs; next came the surgeons of the long robe, who dressed and prescribed for wounds but relegated manipulative operations to the surgeons of the short robe, the barber-surgeons. In addition there were itinerant practitioners, many of them mountebanks, who operated for stones, for hernia, and on the eyes, and who usually resumed their travels in time to escape punishment for butchering their victims.

But Paré, famed for his battlefield achievements, soon left the ranks of the barber-surgeons, and in 1554 was admitted to membership in the Collège de Saint Côme as a surgeon of the long robe. He made many contributions to his chosen field, and personally served four of the kings of France. An example of their esteem for Paré, often accused of Protestantism, was his rescue from the massacre of the Huguenots on St. Bartholomew's Eve in 1572, when King Charles IX hid him in his bedroom. Paré also practiced obstetrics, which during his time was regarded as the exclusive province of the midwives, and he was the first to induce labor artificially by manual means. The practice of midwifery in the Middle Ages is lucidly depicted in the fictional sketch, *Ambroise Paré Does a Delivery*, by Alan F. Guttmacher. In this sketch, Paré does a manual delivery while the midwife looks on in horror and amazement. She rather doubts the wisdom and methods of the great surgeon, and just to ensure success, she falls back on the lore of wine as an antiseptic and also to neutralize the potentially dire effects of Paré's manipulation; therefore, she

... took a mouth full of warm red wine which she spirited into [the infant's] mouth, ears, and nose. ... Madame Grisson [the midwife] lay linen dipped in warm wine to the child's breast and stomach. ... She cleansed his nostrils with small tents dipped in white wine that he might receive the smell. ... [The child] was to receive a warm bath in red wine and water, in which the petals of red roses and the leaves of myrtle had been boiled.[26]

Since the barber-surgeons performed most of the operations, they were the principal users of wine in dressing wounds, a fact apparent from the somewhat meager records left by these generally unlettered practitioners. A letter from the vice-director of New Netherlands in 1658 relates that the barger-surgeons on a single sea voyage, during which there were many accidents and much sickness, "required at least a hogshead or two of French wine and one of brandy."[27]

There was one barber-surgeon of England, the famous Richard Wiseman (1622-1676), who wrote extensively. Like Paré, he won high rank in the medical profession and compiled a textbook of surgery. Although he described himself as a "Water-Drinker," Wiseman wrote of his soldier patients: "I could scarce ever cure any of them without allowing them wine."[28] He directed the use of numerous herbs "to be boiled in Water, or White wine, with an addition of Honey ... in Wounds of the Thorax and Abdomen" and added: "yet they are frequently pre-scribed in all great Wounds."[29] Wiseman described a common battlefield treatment:

> If a Weapon be fastened betwixt two Joynts, make an Ex-tension of Parts both ways . . . that so the Tendons and Liga-ments being stretched, the Weapon may with more ease come out . . . cleanse it from Rags or ought else, and per-mit the Wound to bleed, accordingly as you in your judg-ment shall think fit; still having respect to the Constitution and Habit of body, that what is in the small Veins cut asun-der may flow out, as well to hinder Inflammation as the gen-eration of much Matter. The Bleeding staid, if there be Hair growing about the Wound, shave it off: then wipe away the clotted Bloud with a Sponge dipt in Red wine, Oxycrate, or water.[30]

The foregoing pages represent only an exceedingly brief summary of the role of wine in surgery up to the seventeenth century. As a restorative for surgical patients, wine has served in every age and it is still so employed today. The historical evidence of its effectiveness as an antiseptic is especially remarkable, in view of the greasy ointments that usually were applied with it. Even the Good Samaritan, when he bound up the wounds of the half-dead traveler, "poured in oil and wine." Not until the discoveries of Pasteur inspired Lister to seek true asep-sis was surgery freed from the curse of oily salves. It is interesting to consider, in this respect, the modern find-ings that constitutents other than alcohol, especially in red wine, have bactericidal effects—a subject that will be discussed fully in the closing chapter.

In any case, from the two thousand years of experience thus far reviewed, there is abundant evidence that vast numbers of lives have been saved, and immeasurable human suffering has been assuaged, by the uses of wine in surgery.

BIBLIOGRAPHY

1. See pp. 37, 69.
2. Garrison, F. H.: *An Introduction to the History of Medicine.* Philadelphia, W. B. Saunders Co., 1922, p. 142.
3. See p. 95.
4. Allbutt, Sir T. Clifford: *The Historical Relations of Medicine and Surgery to the End of the Sixteenth Century.* London, Macmillan and Co., Ltd., 1905, pp. 28-31.
5. Gurlt, E.: *Geschichte der Chirurgie.* Berlin, August Hirschwald, 1898, Vol. I, pp. 727, 742.
6. Allbutt: *op. cit.,* p. 30.
7. Walsh: *Old Time Makers of Medicine, op. cit.,* p. 253.
8. Allbutt: *op. cit.,* p. 31.
9. Walsh: *op. cit.,* p. 247.
10. See Chapt. 9, esp. p. 107.
11. Allbutt: *op. cit.,* p. 40.
12. Garrison: *op. cit.,* pp. 146-147.
13. Walsh, J. J.: *Medieval Medicine.* London, A. & C. Beach, Ltd., 1920, p. 140.
14. Garrison: *op. cit.,* p. 148.
15. Arderne, Master John: *De Arte Phisicali et de Cirurgia.* Dated 1412, trans., D'Arcy Power, from transcript by Eric Millar. London, John Bale Sons and Danielsson, Ltd., 1922, p. vii.
16. *Ibid.:* pp. 6-7.
17. *Ibid.:* p. 7.
18. *Ibid.:* p. 30.
19. *Ibid.:* p. 28.
20. Brunschwig, Hieronymus: *The Vertuose Boke of Distyllacyon.* English trans., Laurence Andrew, 1527, pp. 271-273.
21. Allbutt: *op. cit.,* p. 90.
22. Garrison: *op. cit.,* p. 199.
23. Paré, Ambroise: *Apologie and Treatise,* edited and annotated by Francis R. Packard. New York, Paul B. Hoeber, Inc., 1926, pp. 27-28.
24. Garrison: *op. cit.,* p. 219.
25. Paré: *op. cit.,* p. 272. Aegyptiacum was an ointment variously compounded of honey and alum or of vinegar and verdigris. Diacalcitheos was an astringent plaster prepared with oil, litharge, and vitriol.
26. *Bull. Inst. Hist. Med., IV:* 9, pp. 703-717 (1936). In 1961 a similar

ceremony was performed by Henri, pretender to the throne of France. At the christening of his grandson he rubbed the child's lips with raw garlic and washed them with wine.

27. Radbill, Samuel X.: *Bull. Inst. Hist. Med., IV:* 9, p. 717 (1936).

28. Wiseman, Richard, Serjeant-Chirurgeon: *Severall Chirurgicall Treatises*. London, E. Flesher and J. Macock, 1676, p. 346.

29. *Ibid.:* p. 347.

30. *Ibid.:* p. 341. Oxycrate contained vinegar and saffron.

Rise and Fall of the Theriacs

FROM THE MEDICATED WINES of predy-
nastic Egypt came the theriacs of ancient Greece
and Rome, which gave rise first to the cordials
of the monastic alchemists, then to the treacles of medieval and Renaissance Europe, and eventually to the vermouths, bitters, and wine-based tonics of today. Common in their origin, their formulation, and their effects
when ingested, was the menstruum wine. Only an alcoholic vehicle could suspend and dissolve the hodgepodge
of theriac ingredients—vegetable, animal, and mineral;
and wine, with a flavor that masked the taste of medicines, continued to serve this purpose even after the advent of distilled spirits.

As late as the eighteenth century, on the authority of
the ancients, kings and commoners still believed fanati-
cally in the power of the theriacs to alleviate all disorders

ARNALD OF VILLANOVA

AUTHOR OF THE

EARLIEST PRINTED BOOK ON WINE

Courtesy, *Arnald of Villanova: The Earliest Printed Book on Wine.
Now for the first time rendered into English and with an historical
essay by Henry E. Sigerist, M.D., with the facsimile of the original
edition, 1478, New York, Henry Schuman, Ltd.,* 1943, frontispiece.

A PAGE FROM THE

LEECHBOOK OF BALD

Giving recipes for "pain in the joints." Courtesy, Wright, C. E. (ed.):
Bald's Leechbook, British Museum Royal Manuscripts, Facsimile Reproductions, Copenhagen, Rosenkilde and Bagger, 1955, p. 116a.

of body and mind, to subdue the most diverse miseries, to restore perfect vigor, and to confer everlasting youth. The story of these panaceas is a poignant chapter in the history of wine in medicine.

It will be recalled that the original theriac of Nicander, in the second century before Christ, was intended as an antidote to the venomous bites and stings of animals, and that King Mithridates of Pontus compounded mithridatium to counteract the poisons which, in his fear of being murdered, he took daily in order to immunize himself. But the mystic luster attached to these complex medications had such irresistible psychologic appeal that the theriacs were embraced as cures for all ills. In Rome, Celsus and Pliny recorded fantastic claims for their powers, although both also wrote warnings against their indiscriminate use. Galen, on the other hand, naïvely repeated the legend of Mithridates, and especially extolled the newer theriac of Andromachus, which included such key ingredients as opium and the flesh of vipers.

Throughout the Byzantine and Arabic periods the recipes for the miracle medicines were preserved and embellished. The Arabians, among them Haly ben Abbas and Serapion Junior (12th century), wrote extensive commentaries on the Greek and Roman texts dealing with theriacs. Maimonides, when he was appointed by Saladin, Sultan of Egypt, to supervise the preparation of mithridatium for the monarch, became so interested that he wrote a text on the subject.[1] The Arabians attributed to Galen an ingenious experiment to test a theriac: he was described as administering poison to a group of fowls, some of which subsequently received a dose of the antidote. According to the translators, all of the latter survived, but all of the others died.[2]

At the medieval monasteries the early Greek and Roman formulas were copied, and the theriacs, compounded from the plants of the *herbularia*, were dispensed copiously. From the concept of the theriac, the monks evolved the medicinal cordials, which in their original forms, like the ancient panaceas, were essentially mulled wines. Then the alchemists, fanatical believers in the healing powers of metals and precious stones, introduced still more components: gold, ground-up pearls and emeralds, and *aqua vitae*, the spirit of wine.

According to an Anglo-Saxon manuscript of the eleventh century, the theriacs were known in England as early as the ninth century. The manuscript quoted a letter from Helias, Patriarch of Jeruslaem, to King Alfred the Great (849-901), in which Helias recommended:

Theriaca . . . is a good drink for all inward tenderness, and the man who so behaves himself as is here said, he may much help himself. On the day on which he will drink Triacle he shall fast until midday, and not let wind blow on him that day; then let him go to the bath, let him sit there till he sweat; then let him take a cup, put a little warm water in it, then let him take a little bit of the triacle, and mingle with the water, and drain through some thin raiment, then drink it, and let him then go to his bed and wrap himself up warm, and so lie till he sweat well; then let him arise and sit up and clothe himself, and then take his meat at noon (three hours after midday), and protect himself earnestly against the wind that day; then I believe to God it will help the man much.[3]

The high regard in which the theriacs were held by

succeeding English monarchs is evidenced by the fact
that among the precious articles belonging to King Henry
V (1106-1125) was recorded a "Triacle box," and that
it was again mentioned in a "Close Roll" (royal inven-
tory) dating from the reign of King John (1199-1216).[4]

The word "treacle" evolved from *theriaca* with such
earlier spellings as "theriacle," "threacle," "tryacle," and
"triacle," and in the course of time developed an additional and completely different meaning. The transition
was apparently effected by the association of the theriacs with their various modes of administration—as liquids,
electuaries, or lozenges—since each involved the use of
honey or sugar in various degrees of viscosity. When,
following the crusades, sugar was credited with marvelous
medicinal powers and began to replace honey, the drain-
ings of crude sugar, molasses, were sometimes referred
to as treacle, and treacle is still the common term for molasses in England. The association of spiritual and healing power with treacle has persisted in the "brimstone and
treacle" described by Dickens in *Nicholas Nickleby*, and
in the springtime dose of sulfur and molasses administered
to children in modern times.

During the late Middle Ages the center of manufacture
for the theriacs was in Cairo, and it was the custom of the
sultans of Egypt to send gifts of the remedy to the poten-
tates of other countries. At a public ceremony which
took place annually in the Mosque of Morestan, the medicament was mixed by the chief apothecary, who offici-
ated in the presence of the physicians and visitors who
came from throughout Europe to purchase supplies. In
the latter part of the thirteenth century, the Italian cities

of Venice, Pisa, Florence, and Genoa, which controlled the European trade in Oriental drugs and spices, became the centers of theriac manufacture. As at Cairo, elaborate ceremonies accompanied its preparation, preceded by displays of the ingredients in a public square to enable physicians to inspect and approve them. In some cities, as at Montpellier, these formalities and the attendance of illustrious professors of medicine were required by law, in order to assure the public of the virtue of the medicine.

"Venice Treacle" had the highest reputation, being warranted to contain all of the seventy-three substances in the theriac of Andromachus. Much of its fame was due to an astute program of advertising. Each package was wrapped in fine paper, water-marked *Testa d'Oro*, inscribed with the theriac's miraculous powers as a cure for plague, a preventive of contagious diseases of all sorts, a remedy to "chase from the body" all morbid humours, a "cure-all" for the infirmities of the spirit and passions; a "preservative" for those who had suffered the bite of a scorpion, a viper, a mad dog, or any other enraged animal; a useful adjuvant in the treatment of fevers, chronic, putrid, and pestilential; an excellent remedy for illnesses involving the abdominal organs, including stone, gravel, and worms; very good for hydrops, jaundice, consumption and spitting of blood; an "augmentive" of sight; a cure for such internal infirmities of the head as madness, paralysis, apoplexy, epilepsy, trembling and fainting; a "fortifying agent" for diseases of the heart; a curative of leprosy, of delayed menstruation, hemorrhoids, and many other conditions "well enough known to everyone."[5]

In the Decameron of Boccaccio it is recorded that

during the great plague of 1348, the medical faculty of Paris recommended, to prevent the pestilence, "broths with ground pepper, cinnamon and spices . . . a clear, light wine mixed with one sixth water," and "with the meals a little treacle."[6] Although that single epidemic reduced the population of the earth by one fourth, killing more than 500,000 in the Venetian Republic alone, popular faith in the theriacs, including that of Venice, remained firm.

A fifteenth-century English leechbook prescribed treacle "for one alredy infected with ye plage":

Take two onions and cut off the tops, then make a hole in either of them within, fill them with triacle & pep [pepper] & so roast them in the fire whilest it be soft, then take them out and make them clean, which first being stamped, afterward must be strained with four spoonfuls of vinegar and likewise of clean water, then let the patient when it is made blood warm drink it, and lay some of it straight to the sore.[7]

This leechbook, which reflected English medicine of the Tudor period, recommended treacle for every affliction of mankind. For the "biting and stinging of any venomous worm," it directed:

Take an handful of dragance and half a handful of centaury and half so much of rue, and two cloves of garlic; and stamp them small and wring out the juice, and anoint the place that is venomed, and it shall destroy the venom. And if thou drinkest the water of all these distilled and mixed with a little treacle, it will destroy venom within.[8]

"To deliver a man of phlegm," the leechbook advised:

Take three pennyweight of white copperas, three spoonfuls of water, and chafe it a little. And let him drink it a little warm, and colour it with saffron; and give him afterwards when his stomach works, two spoonfuls of aqua vitae, and therein a little treacle. And he shall cast upward what is uppermost, and then it will fret downwards. And then take a hot tile and lay it to his womb, and if any corruption be therein, it shall deliver him.[9]

England produced its own theriac in competition with that of Venice. The rivalry that resulted is revealed in a quaintly phrased pamphlet by Hugh Morgan (1585), apothecary to Queen Elizabeth, in which he stated that the English product

. . . has been compared with other theriacle brought from Constantinople and Venice, and has been better commended. . . . It is very lamentable to consider that straungers doe dayly send into England a false and naughty kinde of Mithridatium and Threacle in great barrelles, more than a thousand weight in a year, and vtter ye same at a lowe price for 3d. and 4d. a pound, to ye great hurt of Her Maiesties subjects and no small gaine to straungers purses.[10]

Queen Elizabeth, who like her father, Henry VIII, was interested in medicine, gave to the London Lord Mayor during the plague of 1594 a prescription of sage, rue, elder leaves, red bramble leaves, ginger, and white wine, a spoonful to be drunk morning and evening for nine days.[11]

In addition to the wine used in their formulation, the theriacs were usually required to be taken with wine. Sir Kenelm Digby (1603-1664), who popularized a "wonderful sympathetic powder" containing mummy flesh and moss from a dead man's skull, advised that the patient be given "one dram for a dose in white wine."[12] Thomas

Lodge, a "Doctor in Phisicke," in his *Treatise of the Plague*, directed that the drink of the afflicted "should consist of good white or claret wine."[13] A sixteenth-century treatise on "Triacles" by William Turner, "Doctor of Physic," discussing the "noble preservative medicine called Mithridatium," described the mode of administration:

> ... I think I shall do well also to declare to such as understand no Latin the virtues, properties, remedies, and helps that may be had of that preservative, which may be taken with much less jeopardy than the great Treacle can be taken ... they that have no ague may take it with wine, or with honeyed wine, or sugared wine, or with spiced wine, if they have a stopped liver. But they that are agueish must take it with water or mead.[14]

The "great Treacle" to which Turner referred was that "called in Latin *Theriaca Andromachi*," and he reccommended it for intestinal worms, diseases of the joints, liver, and spleen, mental disorders, and quartan ague. Even for those in perfect health the treacle was beneficial if used often; and as to epidemic illnesses, it was a preventive:

> A man cannot find a better remedy than this treacle against the pestilence, ... this treacle like a scouring or purging fire will not suffer them that take it in before they be infected, to be infected at all, and delivereth them that are infected already. ... Wherefore I counsel thee, even when thou art in thy best health, to use oft this treacle.[15]

During the reign of James I, Sir Walter Raleigh, then a prisoner in the Tower of London (1603-1616), invented a theriac which eventually became incorporated in the London Pharmacopoeia of 1721 under the title "Confectio Raleighana." It became known as Raleigh's "Sovereign Cordial" or "Royal Cordial" and its virtues were praised by Queen Anne of Denmark and Prince Henry of England. Later its formula was simplified and it was renamed "Confectio Cardiaca." Charles II became curious about Raleigh's cordial and ordered his French apothecary, Le Febre, to prepare a quantity of it from the formula then at hand. It began with forty roots, seeds, and herbs, macerated in spirit of wine, and distilled. With the distillate were combined such additional ingredients as bezoar stones, pearls, coral, deer's horn, amber, musk, antimony, various earths, and sugar.[16] La Wall states that a vestigial remnant of the preparation still remains in modern pharmacopoeias under the name of Aromatic Chalk Powder.[17]

But "Confectio Raleighana" seemed simple when compared to the fabulous theriac of Matthiolus (Pietro Andrea Mattioli, 1501-1577), which embraced no less than two hundred and fifty ingredients. Matthiolus, an Italian commentator of Dioscorides, introduced, among other ingredients, pearls, red coral, emeralds, the powdered parts of vipers, and *Vini veteris albi odorati* [aged white wine], and numbered as single ingredients *Theriacae* and *Mithridatii*, each obviously consisting of many more.[18] In modified form the theriac of Matthiolus became incorporated in the first London Pharmacopoeia (1618), and it was continued as an official remedy until 1746.

The more numerous, rare and costly substances the theriacs were claimed to contain, the greater power they were believed to possess. Since only the rich could afford a remedy as elaborate as that of Matthiolus, a less expensive variety, the *theriaca diatessaron*, was prepared for the poor. Although it contained but five ingredients compounded in wine—gentian, laurel berries, birthwort, juniper berries, and honey—it was warranted an excellent remedy for all fevers and poisons.[19] The fact that the rich could have an elegant theriac of two hundred and fifty ingredients and the poor a modest one of five, both claiming miraculous healing powers, is indicative of the deception practiced during these times. The vast demand for theriacs produced its quota of quacks who peddled completely faked preparations to a gullible public. In 1612 the Master and Wardens of the Grocers' Company of London complained that

... a filthy and unwholesome baggage composition was being brought into this Realm as Tryacle of Genoa, made only of the rotten garble and refuse outcast of all kinds of spices and drugs, hand overhead with a little filthy molasses and tarre to worke it up withal.[20]

Such chicanery was general throughout Europe. When the celebrated French physiologist, Claude Bernard, was an impecunious pre-medical student, he was employed as an apprentice in a Lyons pharmacy. The young man noted that the medicine most in demand was *la Thériaque*. People came from long distances to have their bottles filled, and Bernard would retire to the cellar in order to tap the precious jar in which the compound was stored. The good and simple folk confided to him the multitudinous uses to which they put their allotment of theriac, and the old women said they would not be without it for anything in the world. He anxiously awaited the day when he would be allowed to compound the medicament himself and to discover its secret. When the time came, he was shocked to learn the truth: that remnants, sound or spoiled, of discarded prescriptions in the store were saved and mixed haphazardly in the jug—a medicinal potage—and sold as theriac.

The frauds became so notorious that some physicians, among them Capivaccio, professor at the University of Padua, and Alessandri, physician to the Duke of Savoy, began to question the value of theriacs in general. At first the skeptics were denounced; de Diemerbroeck wrote of them in 1646:

> Let them be silent, who by certain frivolous and twisted arguments and by their criticism of various insignificant points, seek to disparage the virtues of this divine medicament and to banish it from the practice of medicine.[21]

But the critics were not silenced, and the English pharmacists, beset by the growing foreign competition, realized that something decisive was needed to protect their profitable business. They decided that proofs of the value of theriacs should be required, and that fraudulent imports should be discredited and suppressed. It was in response to these moves, aimed against the products of their competitors, that all of the theriacs met their demise in England.

The eminent physician, William Heberden (1710-1801), a scholar of Greek, Hebrew, and Latin, was one of those called upon to express their views. Heberden made a thorough study of the subject, extending from Mithridates to the theriacs of the eighteenth century. In

1745 he reported his findings in an essay entitled *Anti-theriaka.*

Reviewing the history of mithridatium, Heberden showed that the actual formula for the theriac found in the cabinet of the King of Pontus after his death consisted only of twenty leaves of rue, one grain of salt, two nuts, and two dried figs—in shocking contrast to the dozens of exotic substances listed by later authorities. Heberden labeled the "true medicine" of Mithridates as

. . . the numerous, undisciplined forces of a barbarous King, made up of a dissonant crowd collected from different countries, but in reality, an ineffective multitude, that only hinder one another . . . a piece of mere jumble and chance-work without any footsteps of order, proportion or design, without any regard to the known virtues of Simples or to any rules of artful composition.[22]

Not only mithridatium, but all of the other alexipharmic nostrums were ridiculed as absurdities. Heberden especially denounced opium as an ingredient, holding that when the other substances deteriorated by fermentation, the power of the opium was exalted. Finally he stated:

I think that . . . [the] intentions would surely be much better answered [by giving opiates and aromatics] without loading a sick man's stomach with so many other useless things.[23]

When he delivered his report to the College of Physicians, Heberden proposed that both mithridatium and *theriaca* be eliminated from the London Pharmacopoeia, and he demanded an expression of opinion. The resulting ballot indicated how loath the other learned physicians were to part with compounds so long cherished in the minds of the people. His proposal won, thirteen voting in favor of retaining the formulas, and fourteen to expel them.

The onslaught of Herberden ridiculed the theriacs out of existence in England, but they retained their popularity on the continent for another century. As late as 1866, the French *Codex* still listed the formula for the theriac of Andromachus, although its original seventy-three ingredients had been reduced to fifty-seven, and the flesh of vipers was no longer included. And remnants of the theriac recipes still survive in the formulas for modern vermouths and alcoholic bitters, especially in the latter, whose labels describe numerous exotic ingredients and claim multitudinous therapeutic virtues that are reminiscent of the panaceas of antiquity.

The rise and fall of the theriacs encompasses the history of polypharmacy, the compounding of many substances into a single medicine. As polypharmacy declined, those individual substances in the complex recipes which were found to have special value were given permanent places in the materia medica. Wine, as the chief menstruum for the theriacs, and as one of the components which contributed materially to the effects of the nostrums when ingested, was one of these. The demise of the theriacs brought, during the century after Heberden, a substantial increase in the medicinal uses of wine, both unaltered and in various medicated forms.

BIBLIOGRAPHY

1. La Wall, Charles H.: *The Curious Lore of Drugs and Medicines*

(Four Thousand Years of Pharmacy). New York, Garden City Publishing Co., 1927, p. 111.

2. Meunier, Léon: La thériaque. *Bull. Soc. Française d'Hist. Méd.,* III, p. 204 (1904).

3. Wootton: *Chronicles of Pharmacy, op. cit.,* Vol. I, pp. 124, 131-132. Wootton quotes from the manuscript reproduced in *Leechdoms, Wortcunning, and Starcraft,* edited by the Rev. Oswald Cockayne, published in 1864.

4. Thompson, C. J. S.: *The Mystery and Art of the Apothecary.* Philadelphia, J. B. Lippincott Co., 1929, p. 64.

5. Reber, B.: Quelques remarques sur la thériaque, le mithridate, l'opiat de Saloman et l'Orviétan. *Bull. Soc. Française d'Hist. Méd.,* Vol. 13, pp. 471-473 (1914).

6. Quoted by Nohl, J.: *The Black Death.* New York, Harper & Bros., 1924, p. 90.

7. Dawson, W. R.: *A Leechbook, or Collection of Medical Recipes of the Fifteenth Century.* London, Macmillan & Co., Ltd., 1934, p. 339, no. 33, free copy.

8. *Ibid:* p. 57, no. 137.

9. *Ibid.:* p. 219, no. 688.

10. Wootton: *op. cit.,* Vol. II, p. 44.

11. Mullett, Charles F.: *The Bubonic Plague and England.* Lexington, University of Kentucky Press, 1956, p. 97.

12. Robertson, W. G. A.: Digby's receipts. *Ann. Med. Hist.,* 7: 216, p. 218 (1925). Digby was also famed for his use of "viper's wine," and gossip claimed that he poisoned his wife with too frequent doses, which he gave to preserve her beauty.

13. Mullett, Charles F.: The plague of 1603 in England. *Ann. Med. Hist., 9:* 230 ff (1937).

14. Turner, William: "The Book on Treacles" in *A Book of Wines* (1568), Modern English Version. New York, Scholars' Facsimiles and Reprints, 1941, pp. 70-71.

15. *Ibid.:* p. 62.

16. Wootton: *op. cit.,* Vol. I, p. 312.

17. La Wall: *op. cit.,* p. 217.

18. de Diemerbroeck, Isbrandi: *De Peste.* Joannis Iacobi Bibliopolae, 1646, Liber III, Caput V, p. 182.

19. Charas, Moyse: *Pharmacopée Royale Galénique et Chymique.* Paris, 1676, p. 275.

20. Thompson, C. J. S.: *op. cit.* p. 64.

21. de Diemerbroeck: *op. cit.,* p. 179.

22. Heberden, William: *Antitheriaka,* An Essay on Mithridatium and Theriaca. 1745, pp. 9-10, 19.

23. *Ibid.:* p. 16.

CHAPTER

12

The Antidotaria, Formularies, and Pharmacopoeias

NEARLY ALL OF THE BOOKS of therapeutic preparations, from ancient times to the present day, have listed wine prominently among medicinal substances. In fact, the most notable exceptions have been the eight revisions of the Pharmacopoeia of the United States issued since prohibitionist influence reached its height early in the present century. In the antidotaria, formularies, dispensatories, and pharmacopoeias of many countries can be traced much of the history of wine in medicine—its useful employment by countless generations of physicians, its partial eclipse during recent years, and its reappearance among the substances officially recognized in this country as essential in medicine.

It has been shown in previous chapters that wine appeared in the earliest catalogues of healing recipes: the Egyptian medical papyri, the Hindu vedas, and the medical treatises of ancient China. The medicated wines described by Theophrastus in Greece, by Celsus, Pliny, Dioscorides, Columella, and Galen in Rome, and by Avicenna, Maimonides and Mansur during the Arabian period, comprised much of the materia medica of Europe from the Dark Ages until the development of modern experimental medicine.

In each succeeding epoch, recipes for those remedies that had won acceptance in the past were assembled in catalogues of medicinal substances, which in modern times would be called formularies or dispensatories. The European physicians of the Middle Ages, viewing disease as caused by poisons, foul odors, and demons, and naïvely accepting the concept of the theriacs as antidotes, referred to their formularies as "antidotaria." The most noted such work was the *Antidotarium Nicolai* of Salerno, which embraced a catalogue of one hundred and fifty galenicals arranged alphabetically with specific prescriptions for various diseases and a treatise on wines. This antidotarium, written in the twelfth century, was the first formulary to be printed (Venice, 1471).

The chicanery that marked the commerce in theriacs lent particular importance to the specifications and descriptions of drugs given in some of the books of recipes. Their authority was not enough to check the wholesale frauds. In Italy, during the fourteenth century, laws were passed regulating the practices of apothecaries and vintners in order to discourage the counterfeiting of drugs and the watering and adulteration of wine with artificial coloring and sweetening agents.[1] The next step was the adoption of the first pharmacopoeias—formularies establishing standards for drugs with the official authority of publicly recognized bodies—first by local legislatures and eventually, as at present, by national governments.

About 1535 a brilliant young Prussian physician, Valerius Cordus of Erfurt, who took great interest in collecting and improving the formulas of Dioscorides, Galen, Andromachus, Rhazes, Avicenna, and Nicholas of Salerno, assembled them in the *Pharmacorum Conficiendorum Ratio, Vulgo Vocant Dispensatorium*. This volume was used in many of the cities of Saxony, and proved so successful that Valerius Cordus was requested to furnish a copy for the Nuremberg apothecaries. Accordingly he turned over the manuscript to the Senate for examination. When the High Senate of Nuremberg ordered its printing in 1546 and instructed all pharmacists to prepare the medicines according to the *Dispensatorium* of Valerius Cordus, that document became the first real pharmacopoeia. The work of Cordus later was reprinted in thirty-five editions and eight translations, more than any other book of its kind.[2]

The best of the early antidotaria and pharmacopoeias included a good deal of sound hygienic regimen, the legacy of centuries of experience, but also a vast amount of magic, witchcraft, and mysticism. The recipes reflected the folk medicine of the times, and the *Dispensatorium* of Cordus listed, among other ingredients, liver of wolf, lung of fox, spine of deer, white excrement of dog, toothed jaw of pike, wool of sheep, ashes of scorpions

A PHARMACY

OF THE

LATE MIDDLE AGES

The apothecary is serving the customer while his assistant is preparing theriac (Casanatense Library, Rome). Courtesy, Rassegna Medica, vol. XXXVI, No. 2, 1959.

TITLE PAGE OF THE SECOND ISSUE OF THE
PHARMACOPOEIA LONDINENSIS, DECEMBER 7, 1618

The augmented edition is presented as "diligently revised, elaborately
renewed, more correct and more comprehensive." Courtesy, *Pharmacopoeia Londinensis of 1618*, reproduced in facsimile with a Historical
Introduction by George Urdang, Madison, State Historical Society of
Wisconsin, Hollister Pharmaceutical Library, No. 2, 1944, p. 33.

and centipedes, and *Adeps hominis* (body fat of poor sinners).

In medieval England, the collections of recipes—the leechbooks and herbals—contained early Saxon remedies as well as the antidotes popular on the continent. In a fifteenth-century English leechbook mentioned in an earlier chapter are found these prescriptions:

For deafness. Take the white that is amongst ant-hills that is called ant-horses, and let them dry that you may powder them and put it in white wine and put two drops thereof in his ear, and use this a good while.[3]

For the headache that cometh of cold. Seethe betony in wine and wash thine head therein. And it is good for cold of the stomach and for the fumes that rise up into the head.[4]

For aching of teeth. Take figs and cumin and stamp it well together, and boil them well in vinegar or red wine; and make a plaster and lay it to the cheek outside. *Probatum est.*[5]

Ache by the bone, and all manner of bruises. Take a good quantity of wormwood and cut into three or four parts, and boil it in the best wine that you may have. . . . And put therein a piece of new woollen cloth . . . wrap the sore therein, and do thus oft and always hot, and he shall be whole by God's grace.[6]

John of Gaddesden (*ca.* 1280-1361), the physician to King Edward II and the original "Doctor of Physic" in Chaucer's poem, prepared a pharmaceutical compendium entitled the *Rosa Anglica*. As a cure for blindness he listed wine of fennel and parsley, a relic of the ancient Saxon belief in fennel as one of the nine sacred herbs powerful against the nine venoms, or causes of disease.[7] Gaddesden also ascribed special virtues to unmedicated wine, writing that it "prevents the food from swimming about the stomach, dispenses the flatulence, provokes the urine and the sweat; and helps nature to expel excess matter." [8]

An *Herball* published in 1525 by a London printer, Richard Banckes, popularized nutmeg and mace as medications in England with such prescriptions as these:

... for a cold stomach that is feeble of digestion and for the liver, give him wine that nutmegs is boiled in. Also good for the same, boil nutmegs and mastic in wine and drink it. This is good for disease in the stomach and in the bowels to break wind. For a cold stomach that may not defy nor digest well, take maces and boil them in wine and drink it .... if thou be feeble with unkindly sweat, take and boil well the leaves [of rosemary] in clean water, and when the water is cold, put thereto as much of white wine, and then make therein sops and eat thou well thereof, and thou shall recover appetite. [9]

English physicians also composed manuals of diet and behavior for their individual patients. The following advice was addressed by Dr. Conrad Heingarten, in 1480, to the Duchess of Bourbon, the daughter of King Charles VII:

The proper drink is white wine or red wine of thin consistency with a bouquet and notably hot and dry. And let her above all shun the use of water. [10]

In another epistle, of 1663, Dr. Richard Andrews directed the pregnant Countess of Newcastle:

When you are in travail I would have you take powder of cassia, saffron and borax as much as will lie upon a groat on a spoonful of burnt white wine. [11]

Vermouth was listed among the medicinal wines in

the German medical text of Dr. Johannes Dryander (d. 1560). He described "vermouth wine" as "very good for old age, both for the cold and the hot tempers . . . it gets rid of bad breath due to stomach upset and stimulates the liver and the pancreas. It improves the skin and the complexion and it is to be drunk before and after eating." Dryander devoted an entire chapter to wine as an aid to health.[12]

During the sixteenth century, Paracelsus espoused the pharmaceutic uses of iron and antimony. The usual method of preparing the former was to immerse iron filings or iron wire in wine, allowing the mixture to stand for a period of weeks while the metal rusted. As a remedy for anemia, this *vinum ferri* was popular until the late nineteenth century. Wine of antimony, admitted in 1637 to the published list of remedies in France, continues in use at present as a diaphoretic, expectorant, and emetic.[13]

The first London Pharmacopoeia, published in 1618, incorporated a number of theriacs, three medicated wines, ten medicated vinegars, more than two hundred of the medicated waters invented by Arnald of Villanova three centuries earlier, and several hundred other substances, including oils of ants, earthworms, and vitriol; lozenges of vipers with plasters of live frogs and worms, and precious stones reduced to powders. After various reprintings a second edition was published in 1650, wherein several preparations were deleted and new ones added, including antimonial wine prepared from the regulus of antimony. Among the remedies retained were *liquor crani humani*, prepared from moss grown on "the skull of a man killed by violence," prescribed for "falling sickness," gout, apoplexy, and the somnolency; powdered human bone in red wine as a cure for dysentery, and water distilled from human hair and mixed with honey to promote the growth of hair. The edition of 1677 added steel wine, Peruvian bark, crabs' eyes, human urine, and *Aqua Vitae Hibernorum sive Usquebagh* (Irish whiskey).

In 1741 there appeared in London a *Pharmacopoeia officinalis & extemporanea; or, A Compleat English Dispensatory*, which contained the following formula:

Vinum Millepedum (Hog-Lice Wine).—Take hog-lice, half a pound, put them alive into two pounds of white port wine, and after some days' infusion strain and press out very hard; then put in saffron two drachms, salt of steel one drachm, and salt of amber two scruples, and after three or four days strain and filter for use. This is an admirable medicine against the jaundice, dropsy or any cachectic habit. It greatly deterges all the viscera, and throws off a great deal of superfluous humours by urine. It may be given twice a day, two ounces at a time.[14]

Other European pharmacopoeias were published during the seventeenth and eighteenth centuries: that of Amsterdam in 1636, Paris in 1639, Spain in 1651, Brussels in 1671, and Russia in 1778. The first national pharmacopoeia was the *Codex medicamentarius* of France, which appeared in 1819. In Spain, the most widely used pharmacopoeia was that of Madrid, issued in 1729, which in its second edition ten years later listed a remarkable group of preparations with opium, including *Laudanum Liquidum* with saffron, cinnamon, cloves, and white wine.

After Heberden exposed mithridatium in 1745, the theriacs were gradually dropped from successive editions of the pharmacopoeias, and the numbers of simpler preparations employing wine or alcohol increased markedly. *Thomson's London Dispensatory*, published in 1818, contained ten formulas for medicated wines and an extensive chapter on wines and their medicinal properties and uses. Wine of socotorine aloes was listed as "long employed with benefit in cold, phlegmatic habits, paralysis, gout, dyspepsia and chlorosis"; wine of ipecac as a remedy for coughs and dysentery; wine of tobacco for "dropsies and ileus," and wine of opium for inflammation of the eyes. In 1835, the *Pharmacopoeia Universalis* of Heidelberg listed a total of one hundred and seventy wines. The London Pharmacopoeia of 1836 described wine of aloes as a stomachic and purgative; wine of meadow saffron as a diuretic and a specific in gout, "allaying the pain and cutting short the paroxysm"; wine of ipecac as a diaphoretic and emetic, better adapted for infants than wine of antimony; and wine of white hellebore as an emetic and cathartic, "acting usually with considerable violence." Each of the latter recipes specified sherry as the wine to be used. The *Pharmacopée Universelle* of Paris in 1840 listed one hundred and sixty-four wines, including wines of gentian, of mustard, of rhubarb, of saffron, and of squill. The *Pharmacopeae Suecicae* of Sweden in 1869 catalogued fifteen wines, including malaga, port, and sherry.

The first Pharmacopoeia of the United States, published at Boston in 1820, contained formulas for nine *vina medicata*. Among them appeared the following:

Vinum Ferri (Wine of Iron). Take of Iron Wire cut in pieces, four ounces. Wine, four pints. Sprinkle the wire with two pints of the wine, and expose it to the air until it be covered with rust; then add the rest of the wine; macerate for ten days, with occasional agitation, and filter.

Vinum Ipecacuanhae (Wine of Ipecac). Take of Ipecacuanha bruised, two ounces. Wine, two pints. Macerate for ten days, and strain.

Vinum Opii (Wine of Opium, called Sydenham's Laudanum). Take of opium, two ounces; Cinnamon, bruised; Cloves, bruised, each one drachm. Wine, one pint. Macerate for ten days, and strain.

Vinum Tabaci (Wine of Tobacco). Take of tobacco, one ounce. Wine, one pint. Macerate for ten days, and filter.

Similar formulas were given for wines of aloes, of tartarized antimony, of meadow saffron, of rhubarb, of white hellebore, and of compound wine of gentian. The recipes for the rhubarb and gentian wines called for alcohol in addition to the wine. Alcohol, diluted and ammoniated, was listed, but wine was the only alcoholic beverage included in this edition.

In 1830, at a general convention held in New York to revise the first edition of the Pharmacopoeia, provision was made for subsequent revisions every ten years. The 1830 revision added *Alcohol officinale*, which it described as "a powerful diffusible stimulant; principally employed as an external application, and for pharmaceutic purposes." *Vinum* (wine) was specified as the product of *Vitis vinifera*, the European wine grape. Under the subhead "Medicinal Operations," wine "when pure, and properly matured," was described as "stimulant, tonic, antispasmodic, nutritive."

Gradually more wines were added to the pharmacopoeial lists in both this country and England. The British

Pharmacopoeia of 1885 contained, among other wines, a standard for sherry and formulas for wines of citrate of iron, of colchicum corm, of orange, and of quinine, and also for *spiritus vini gallici*, which was defined as French brandy. The 1850 *United States Pharmacopoeia* added *Vinum Portense* (port) and *Vinum Xericum* (sherry), and also brandy and *Spiritus Frumenti* (whiskey). In 1883 standards were introduced for *Vinum Album* (unmedicated white wine), *Vinum Album Fortius* (stronger white wine, 20 to 25 per cent alcoholic content by weight), *Vinum Rubrum* (unmedicated red wine), and *Vinum Aromaticum*, a mixture with lavender, origanum, peppermint, rosemary, sage, and wormwood. The 1883 revision deleted port, sherry, and wine of tobacco, and in 1893 "stronger white wine" was eliminated.

In 1883 there appeared a *Therapeutic Handbook of the United States Pharmacopoeia*, by D. Robert T. Edes, professor of materia medica at Harvard, who stated in the foreword that the book was prepared at the suggestion of the president of the revisional convention. Edes discussed the wines of various countries, warning particularly against those that were adulterated. Of *Vinum Album* he wrote:

The action of wine is essentially that of alcohol, modified by the ethers and oils contained in it when duly aged. Wine is at first more stimulating than alcohol alone, but after a time its effects correspond closely enough to those of alcohol in the same degree of dilution. Wine is used in medicine for the general purposes of alcohol, being preferred, however, to the stronger forms in dyspeptic disorders, as a cardiac stimulant, and in those cases of acute and typhoidal diseases where large doses are not required. For strictly dietetic purposes the wines weaker than the officinal strength are largely used, and are in most cases decidedly preferable.

Edes described *Vinum Aromaticum* as "a stimulant and bitter which may be used as a tonic in gastric debility and dyspepsia." Of *Vinum Rubrum* he wrote:

. . . in the diarrhoea of typhoid, for instance, it may be substituted for sherry, instead of administering with the sherry, as a drug, some other astringent, like catechu or logwood.[15]

By 1905, when the eighth revision of the *United States Pharmacopoeia* was issued, the number of medicinal wines totaled twelve: unmedicated white and red wines and wines of antimony, of coca, of colchicum corm, of colchicum seed, of ergot, of ferric citrate, of ipecac, of iron, of iron bitter, and of opium.

During the first decade of this century, while Carry Nation and her hatchet smashed saloons, the prohibition movement reached its height, drying up cities, towns, and entire states as its leaders aimed at the final extinction of "the demon rum" in America. One of the defenses against prohibition offered by the beleaguered beverage industries was that their products were officially recognized as medicines. In order to demolish this argument, the dry forces aimed well-financed campaigns of political pressure at the Pharmacopoeia listings of wines and spirits. Their targets, lacking modern experimental proofs of their therapeutic efficacy, were vulnerable, and the prohibitionists were easily victorious. The Pharmacopoeial Convention of 1916 voted to delete all twelve of the wines that appeared in the 1905 edition, as well as whiskey and brandy.

The *Bulletin of Pharmacy*, commenting on the expulsion of the ancient remedies, stated that the medicinal wines

. . . were the forerunners of the tinctures, and maintained their place for years because of the vinous odor and flavor. They have no advantages over the corresponding tinctures and are gradually passing into history.[16]

The *Practical Druggist* was more emphatic:

The deletion of wines from the U. S. P. is stated to be one of the wise acts of the Revision Committee, as a more useless and a less uniform class of galenicals cannot well be imagined.[17]

International agreements were negotiated, providing that no potent medicament should be prepared in the form of a medicinal wine. And when the *British Pharmacopoeia* was revised in 1932, it, too, dropped the wines it had listed for three hundred years. Subsequent editions contained instructions to pharmacists, directing that when the medicated wines were prescribed or demanded, the corresponding elixirs or tinctures should be dispensed instead.

The intensity of the anti-alcohol crusade was such that it reached the *National Formulary*, the collection of medicinal specifications and recipes issued by the American Pharmaceutical Association. The Formulary, which in 1916 listed standards for sherry and for fifteen medicated wines (wine of antimony, compound wine of orange, wines of beef, of beef and iron, of colchicum corm, of colchicum seed, of iron, bitter wine of iron, wines of white ash, of ipecac, of pepsin, of tar, of wild cherry, ferrated wine of wild cherry, and wine of rhubarb),[18] dropped them all in 1926, substituting elixirs and tinctures calling for the use of alcohol instead of wine.

The privately published *United States Dispensatory*, which in 1905 had recommended red wine as a tonic and as an antidiarrheic agent in convalescence, reduced its listings of wines from seventeen in that edition to eight in 1926, and eliminated them completely in 1937.[19]

Exclusion from the official books of medicinal standards, however, did not put an end to the prescription of wines and spirits as medicine. Instead, since the prohibition law specifically permitted the manufacture of alcoholic beverages for medicinal uses, physicians prescribed them in volumes never equaled before or since—more often for festive than for therapeutic purposes. Prescription liquor was further legitimized in 1926 by the restoration of whiskey and brandy to the Pharmacopoeia, where they remained through the 1936 and 1942 editions, being finally deleted in 1947. The manufacturers of pharmaceutical preparations continued to employ wines as menstruums for such essential preparations as vitamins, tonics, and stomachic bitters. There also was a phenomenal rise in the sales of proprietary wine tonics, which appeared in unprecedented numbers with fanciful new names and advertising; and although the Prohibition Bureau required these products to be medicated sufficiently to make them unpalatable, millions of thirsty Americans found them an acceptable tipple.

Following the repeal of prohibition in 1933, the continuing need for pharmaceutical standards for wine brought belated action by the American Pharmaceutical

Association to restore the essential definitions to the *National Formulary*. Standards for port and sherry were considered, but after extended discussion only sherry was accepted. This was unfortunate since port, too, is used in a number of medicinal preparations. In the 1946 edition of the Formulary the following definitions reappeared:

Vinum Xericum (Sherry Wine) is an alcoholic liquid obtained by fermenting the juices of sound, ripe grapes, fortifying with brandy, and containing, at $15.56°$, not less than 17 per cent and not more than 24 per cent, by volume, of C_2H_5OH.

Caro, Ferrum et Vinum (Beef, Iron and Wine) contains in each 100 cc., an amount of ferric ammonium citrate corresponding to not less than 0.75 gm. and not more than 0.975 gm. of iron.[20]

Also returned to the Formulary after their thirty-year absence were the standards for whiskey and brandy.[21]

In the 1955 *United States Pharmacopoeia*, alcohol was described as a "pharmaceutic necessity," but for some reason these words were deleted from the revision of 1960. Both editions refer quaintly to alcohol as *spiritus vini rectificatus*, although no *vini* are to be found.

One result of the pharmacopoeial reticence concerning wine is the peculiar practice in the labeling of certain pharmaceutical preparations—in which all other components are required to be shown—of concealing the fact that they are compounded in wine. This has tended to obscure the fact that virtually all of the liquid vitamin formulas have been prepared in solutions of white wine. Firms supplying the neurophosphate and blood tonics

have also made increasing use of detannated wines as preferred menstruums for these products. One of the most
effective medications for severe cases of Parkinson's disease is Bulgarian belladonna root suspended in white
table wine (for which no standards appear in either the
Pharmacopoeia, the Formulary, or the Dispensatory), and
repeated tests have shown that the results attained with
the table wine extract could not be duplicated when
dilute alcohol was substituted for the wine.[22] Many in
the pharmaceutical industry are becoming aware that the
mild acidity, the buffering action, the desirable range of
alcoholic content, and the pleasant flavor provided by
the aromatic organic esters are qualities that combine to
make wine preeminent among all the vehicles of organic
acid nutrients.

Most other national pharmacopoeias, except the Brit-
ish, have continued to list medicinal wines. The French
Codex of 1960 lists seven, and the *Farmacopea Ufficinale*
of Italy has standards for six. The 1958 edition of the
German text, *Hagers Handbuch der Pharmazeutischen
Praxis*, contains separate chapters on *Vinum* and *Vina
Medicata*, cataloguing some forty-one medicated wines.
The 1952 Pharmacopoeia of Japan lists wine, while mak-
ing no mention of that country's national beverage, sake.

Obviously, the continued exclusion of wine from the
United States Pharmacopoeia and its present skimpy recognition in the *National Formulary* result from the modern assumption that the medicinal values attributed to
this beverage during the past four thousand years have
been due solely to its content of alcohol. Only in recent
years has it been shown that the non-alcoholic compo-

nents of wines possess many of the physiologic and psychophysiologic values empirically observed by the ancients—that wine is much more than an aqueous alcoholic solution.

Quite possibly, as the new experimental and clinical evidence of these values continues to accumulate, some future meetings of the Pharmacopoeial Convention and of the Committee on the National Formulary will take note thereof, and will amplify the recognition given wines in the official books of medicinal substances.

BIBLIOGRAPHY

1. The origins of many of the complex laws and regulations that govern the production and cellar treatment of pure wines can be traced to the early pharmacopoeial standards that were adopted to protect the users of wine as medicine.

2. Peters, Hermann: *Pictorial History of Ancient Pharmacy*. Trans. from the German, revisions and additions by Wm. Netter, 3rd ed., Chicago, G. P. Engelhard and Co., 1906, p. 129.

3. Dawson: *A Leechbook, op. cit.*, p. 101, no. 268.

4. *Ibid.*: p. 21, no. 14.

5. *Ibid.*: p. 25, no. 29.

6. *Ibid.*: p. 35, no. 61.

7. Wootton: *Chronicles of Pharmacy, op. cit.*, Vol. I, p. 134.

8. Jones, Ida B.: Popular medical knowledge in fourteenth century English literature. *Bull. Inst. Hist. Med.*, V: 6, p. 563 (1937).

9. Banckes, Richard: *An Herball*. Edited and trans. into modern English and introduced by Sanford V. Larkey and Thomas Pyles, New York, Scholars' Facsimiles & Reprints, 1941, pp. 52-53, 50, 70.

10. Thorndike, Lynn: Conrad Heingarten in Zurich manuscripts, especially his advice to the Duchess of Bourbon. *Bull. Inst. Hist. Med., IV*: 2, pp. 81-87 (1936)

11. Ruhräh, John: Notes on English medicine. *Ann. Med. Hist., 3*: 308 (1931).

12. Dryander, Johannes: *Der Gantzen Arzenei Gemeyner Inhalt.* Frankfurt, C. Egenolph, 1542, pp. 36-42.

13. Peters (*op. cit.*, pp. 140-141) states that in the monasteries during the seventeeth century, monks addicted to wine were compelled to drink from antimony goblets. The wine dissolved the antimony, causing nausea and creating an aversion to drink—a forerunner of the modern conditioned reflex treatment of alcoholics.

14. *Ibid.:* p. 142.

15. Edes, Robert T.: *Therapeutic Handbook of the United States Pharmacopoeia.* New York, William Wood and Co., 1883, pp. 349-353.

16. *Bull. Pharm., 30:* 365 (1916).

17. *Pract. Drug. & Spatula, 34:* 26 (1916).

18. All of the recipes for medicated wines in the 1916 Formulary call for their preparation with sherry. However, the three preceding editions (1888, 1896, and 1906) specified variously the use of angelica, claret, port, white wine, and "stronger white wine."

19. The Dispensatory in its 1950 edition again listed sherry, because of its use as an ingredient of beef, iron and wine.

20. In the 1960 edition, the Latin names were deleted, and the titles appear as "Sherry" and "Beef, Iron and Wine."

21. The *National Formulary* is quoted in federal and state laws as having equal authority with the Pharmacopoeia.

22. See pp. 198-199.

The Universal Medicine— and Its Eclipse

THROUGHOUT THE SEVENTEENTH, eighteenth, and nineteenth centuries, while important advances were being made in the basic biologic sciences, the treatment of disease was still largely a matter of clinical acumen. The post-Renaissance clinicians, aiming at palliatives and cures, were guided in great part by trial and error in their choice of medication. Tradition also had its influence; they logically employed those remedies with the longest pedigrees of ancient recommendation. But the use of most medicines was still an art and not yet a science, and continued generally in the ways established by ancient and medieval physicians. The prescription of wine, with its imposing record as a therapeutic agent, was almost universal, and reached its highest point in medical history during these times. Here was an important stimulant of appetite, an effective diuretic, and a reliable sedative; a nutritious and pleasant dietary beverage, usually beneficial or at least relatively harmless in most organic disorders, and capable of producing dramatic recoveries in psychosomatic disturbances.

During this period the different kinds of wine had their special uses: the astringent red wines for diarrhea, the white wines as diuretics, port in acute fevers and for anemia, claret and burgundy for anorexia, champagne for nausea and catarrhal conditions, and port, sherry, and madeira in convalescence. This was the general pattern, although the prescriptions of individual physicians varied. The pharmacies of the hospitals stocked large assortments of wines and dispensed them copiously. The records of the Alice Hospital in Darmstadt, Germany, disclosed that during a period of less than six months, betwen October, 1870, and early April 1871, there were used 4,633 bottles of white and 6,332 of red rhenish wine, 60 bottles of champagne, a few dozens of superior white wine, a few of Bordeaux, and about 30 dozen of port. The number of patients admitted during the period was 755.[1] A list of the dietaries of English hospitals compiled by Dr. F. W. Pavy in 1875 referred to wine, brandy, gin, and porter as "extras," and specified that in the diets for children under ten years of age, these beverages were "to be served when specially ordered, such order being renewed at each regular visit of the physician or surgeon."[2]

The contraindications were few; most of the standard

treatments for general debility, typhoid fever, diphtheria, and even for tuberculosis, called for the prescription of wine. Its medical use was often excessive, and it was bitterly opposed by the temperance crusaders of nineteenth-century England and America. The eventual reaction against the ancient medicine was therefore inevitable, when the modern synthetic drugs arrived.

Some of the curative powers attributed to the beverage made it a veritable fetish. Dr. Nathaniel Hodges, recording his experiences while caring for the afflicted throughout the London plague epidemic of 1665, credited sherry-sack with saving his life. He drank the wine before and after his meals, sucking lozenges of myrrh, cinnamon, and angelica root during the day, and "concluded the evening at home, by drinking to cheerfulness of my old favorite liquor, which encouraged sleep and an easy breathing through all the pores all night." On two occasions he felt ill and feared he might be smitten with the pestilence, but each time a glass of sherry-sack proved a sure preventive.[3]

Wine was called "the Grand Preserver of Health and Restorer in Most Diseases." This was the descriptive subtitle of a work by "a Fellow of the Colleges," published in London in 1724. Quoting from numerous unnamed physicians, as well as from their patients, this volume related cures of smallpox and malignant fevers with "warm canary" wine, and declared that

. . . wine, prudently used, has naturally a strong and direct Tendency to prolong Life and prevent Diseases. . . . Wine of it self is a very wholesome Liquor; and cures even our

Vices, and the Distemper of the Soul; and fits us for the Offices of Life . . . [it] is also a Preservative from Venereal Infection, being used internally as well as externally.[4]

William Heberden, whose exposure of mithridatium in 1745 ended the popularity of the theriac in England, employed wine more conservatively, advocating it as well as spirituous cordials for the relief of pain in angina pectoris. Heberden, incidentally, was famous for a strange medicine of his own invention, the *Mistura Ferri Aromatica.* It contained various vegetable substances and half an ounce of iron filings, presumably compounded in wine or spirit.[5]

Those physicians who wrote of wine did so cautiously, taking care to emphasize moderation. Dr. William Sandford, surgeon to the Worcester Infirmary, published *A Few Practical Remarks on the Medicinal Effects of Wine and Spirits*, with "observations on the oeconomy of health, intended principally for the use of parents, guardians, and others intrusted with the care of youth." He advocated its use, but only "within certain limits":

Wine . . . is undoubtedly one of those real blessings with which a kind Providence has favored us; and its true uses and effects have long been known, and considered, by medical writers of very high eminence and authority . . . with regard to the uses of wine, and its good effects on the human body in certain states of indisposition, especially, where the persons have not been in the habit of daily using it:—to such it proves particularly beneficial when taken in moderate quantity, as its tendency is to increase the circulation of the fluids, and to stimulate all the functions of the mind and body. . . . And this was probably the principal reason that wine, when first introduced medicinally as a cordial into this kingdom, was sold only by the apothecaries, which we are well assured it was about the year 1300. . . . Wine quickens the pulse, raises the spirits, and gives more than common animation *for the time;* but no sooner has the intoxicating delirium ceased than the patient becomes weak, enervated, and depressed in mind and body: here we distinctly see both the stimulant and sedative powers of wine. . . .[6]

Dr. Sandford especially praised the wine of Madeira, stating that it "abounds in the truest vinous elements; it is a most potent stimulant to the nerves," and that because of its low tartar content, "most probably it is that invalids . . . with depraved appetites, and weak stomachs disposed to acidity, find it to agree with them better than other wines."[7]

A London physician, Dr. Alexander Henderson, in 1824 wrote a history of wine, in which he flatly opposed any use of the beverage except as medicine. He discoursed at length on "the deplorable effects of the abuse of wine, from which all the exhortations of the moralist, and all the care of the legislator, have been insufficient to preserve mankind." But then he cautiously added:

It must be acknowledged, however, that the natives of wine-countries, with the exception, perhaps, of the Greeks and Persians, are much less prone to intemperance, than those nations for whom the attraction of vinous liquors seems to increase, in proportion as they recede from the climates that produce them.[8]

Warning against excessive consumption, he also testified to the esteem in which wine was held as a therapeutic agent:

Although, when drunk without restraint, wine can only

be considered a "delightful poison," as the Persians, who know it chiefly by its abuse, have appropriately termed it, yet, like other poisons, when administered with judgment and discretion, it is capable of producing the most beneficial effects. Temperately used, it acts as a cordial and stimulant; quickening the action of the heart and arteries, diffusing an agreeable warmth over the body, promoting the different secretions, communicating a sense of increased muscular force, exalting the nervous energy, and banishing all unpleasant feelings from the mind. Even in this light, it is to be viewed rather as a medicine than as a beverage adapted to common use; for a person in sound health can require no such excitement of his frame, and, by frequently inducing this state of preternatural strength, he must, sooner or later, exhaust the vital powers.[9]

Having advised against the "common" use of wine, Henderson than itemized some of its specific uses in treating disease. He recommended rhine and moselle wines for their dietetic properties, stating:

In certain species of fever, accompanied by a low pulse and great nervous exhaustion, they have been found to possess considerable efficacy, and may certainly be given with more safety than most other kinds; as the proportion of alcohol in them is small, and its effects are moderated by the presence of free acids. They are also said to be of service in diminishing obesity.[10]

Discussing the other wines commonly prescribed, he conceded that "the wines of Oporto, which abound in the astringent principle, and derive additional potency from the brandy added to them previous to exportation, may be serviceable in disorders of the alimentary canal, where gentle tonics are required." He preferred madeiras to sherries as "the best adapted to invalids . . . [these wines] agreeing better with dyspeptic habits." Dr. Henderson also defended the wines of Champagne against the accusation that they caused gout, stating that this "seems to be contradicted by the infrequency of that disorder in the province where they are made."[11]

The attacks on the medical profession by the crusaders against alcohol became so virulent that relatively few physicians dared to write on the subject. In 1851 a prize was awarded to Dr. William B. Carpenter, a professor of medical jurisprudence in University College, London, for an essay in which he defended his wine-prescribing colleagues. He wrote:

> Those who maintain . . . that, in fact, Alcohol is to almost everyone a true *poison*, slower or more rapid in its operation, according to the rate at which it is taken,—may still maintain with perfect consistency, that (like many other poisons) it may be a most valuable *remedy*, when administered with caution and discrimination, in various forms of disease.[12]

In 1862, the following statement appeared in a wine manual by Charles Tovey:

> Modern practitioners do not appear to advocate the use of wine as a medicine to the same extent as the ancient physicians. Some dislike to give a professional sanction to what may be termed the gratification of a depraved taste, and fear that a habit formed during illness may be continued in convalescence. . . .[13]

Evidently the English physicians exercised discrimination in choosing among the different qualities of wine for their patients, for between 1863 and 1865, the *Medical Times and Gazette* published an entire series of articles by Dr. Robert Druitt on the relative merits of foreign wines. In 1873 the series appeared in book form, entitled *A Report on the Cheap Wines from France, Germany, Italy, Austria, Greece, Hungary, and Australia—Their Use in Diet and Medicine*. He denounced "the wine forgeries of Hamburg," recommending old sherry as a heart stimulant and stomachic, clarets for the gouty and for measles in children, and champagne for neuralgia and influenza. "The medical practitioner," he wrote, ". . . should know the virtues of wine as an article of diet for the healthy, and should prescribe what, when, and how much should be taken by the sick."[14]

The medical profession was directly accused of promoting drunkenness, in a *History of Drink* by James Samuelson, barrister-at-law:

> Another explanation has been given of the prevalence of drunkenness, namely, the practice on the part of medical men of too freely prescribing alcohol as a remedy for bodily ailments. . . . indeed, we shall find presently that medical men of the higher order admit this to be the case. The downfall of many a man or woman has dated from the first dose prescribed by a heedless or mercenary physician.[15]

Although Samuelson devoted his entire volume to a recital and condemnation of the evils of alcohol, he nevertheless admitted "the necessary employment of alcohol in cases of disease, for we must be careful not to pronounce an opinion which shall cause unnecessary suffering to the innocent and afflicted . . ."[16] On this point the barrister quoted an eloquent letter written to him by Dr. Savory, of St. Bartholomew's Hospital:

> Although I am willing to admit that in my opinion alcohol, in its various forms of wine, beer, and spirits, is often

needlessly and recklessly prescribed in the practice of surgery, yet I am sure that we could not altogether dispense with its use without frequent disadvantage to our patients, and even the occasional sacrifice of life. In cases where stimulants are required, sometimes others, as certain drugs, might be substituted for those, either without loss or with positive gain; but, after full allowance is made for this, there must remain, I think, many instances in which alcoholic drinks largely promote recovery, and several in which the balance of life and death turns upon their prompt and judicious administration. When I reflect on the enormous evil of alcohol to the community—an evil in its physical and moral results beyond parallel—I wish with all my heart that I could, as a surgeon, say less for this most prolific parent of disease and crime."[17]

During the 1870's, Dr. Francis Anstie, editor of the *Practitioner* and physician to Westminster Hospital in London, prepared the most comprehensive set of directions for the medical prescription of wine thus far compiled. It appeared originally as a series of articles in the *Practitioner* and in 1877 was published in book form, bearing the title *On the Uses of Wine in Health and Disease.*[18] Dr. Anstie summarily dismissed the opponents of wine, declaring that its medical use was "established . . . by wide-spread custom" and therefore not subject to discussions of "lawfulnesss or . . . advisability." He criticized the haphazard manner in which dissimilar wines were being administered by his colleagues for different ailments, stating that "it [is] common to meet with invalids and others who have received diametrically opposite directions as to the choice of beverages from different practitioners of equal standing." He had various wines chemically analyzed at Westminster Hospital for their content of alcohol, sugar, fixed and free acids, and ash. In discussing the results, he admonished his fellow physicians to be guided thereby, instead of by their "prejudices . . . commercial motives . . . , [and] the many trade circulars which have been published under the guise of scientific pamphlets on wine."

He drew sharp distinctions between "the *strong* wines, including port, sherry, madeira, marsala, and all that genus" and the "light wines , . . . namely, [those] that average no more than 10 per cent of alcoholic strength," maintaining that the place of the former was "rather among the cordials, to be used under expressed and careful medical sanction. . . ." For daily use by healthy adults, he insisted that wines should contain "not . . . more than 10 per cent absolute alcohol: 8 or 9 per cent is better." But for children, "where a tendency to wasting is very marked," and "of course always under medical sanction," he recommended

. . . precisely the reverse of the plan which is appropriate for adults. The latter [adults] should be advised to take wine only with their meals, and the problem, therefore, is to find for them a light natural wine which may safely be used as a beverage. With children, on the contrary, it is much better to give wine at separate hours, as if it were strictly a medicine; and the potent wines, disguised and made somewhat disagreeable by the addition of bitters, are much the best: for example, a teaspoonful of sherry or port made up to a tablespoonful with strong infusion of gentian, which might be given three times a day to a child of three or four years old . . . .

For the aged, too, he specified the stronger wines:

As a dietetic aid in the debility of old age the more potent wines are even more remarkably useful than in infancy and childhood. More particularly in the condition of sleeplessness, attended often with slow and inefficient digestion, and a tendency to stomach cramps, a generous and potent wine is often of great value. It is not desirable for such persons to include a large allowance of fluid in their daily diet, and their alcohol may well be taken in the more concentrated forms. . . . One very important effect of the highly etherized wines, which are at the same time of rather high alcoholic strength, is their power to produce tranquil and prolonged sleep in aged persons. . . . Plain alcohol is . . . a much less efficient hypnotic . . . .

Dr. Anstie devoted half of his book to "the uses of wine in health," and the remainder, in two sections, to its uses in acute and in chronic diseases. For the healthy, "the moderate diners-out, and the virtuous dancing young ladies," he advised that

. . . half a bottle a day of . . . [light] wine for a sedentary, and a bottle a day for a vigorous and actively employed adult, affords a reasonable and prudent allowance of alcohol; and this quantity of wine, either alone or with water, will be enough to satisfy the needs of moderate persons for a beverage at lunch and dinner, the only two meals at which alcohol should, as a rule, be taken.

Deploring "the multiplication of alcoholic drinks which are taken by the richer classes," he wrote:

It is therefore much to be desired that people may be educated in the direction of using only one alcoholic drink; at least for every-day consumption . . . adherence to one drink, and generally one *wine*, is almost a necessity for the purposes of health.

In acute diseases, Dr. Anstie prescribed plain diluted alcohol, rather than wine, during persistent "high temperature, . . . delirium, or other evidences of nervous prostration, great rapidity with a high degree of dicrotism of the pulse, and especially a tendency of the latter to become unrhythmical," and also in pneumonia and bronchitis without a high fever. But "in the later stages of severe febrile disease with great exhaustion of the heart, especially when combined with sleeplessness," he preferred "the ethereal constituents of wine . . . [of] low alcoholic strength . . . , together with the presence of carbonic acid, as in the finer effervescing wines. . . ." For patients in the third and fourth weeks of typhoid fever, he recommended old sherry as ideal:

. . . we shall, I believe, do best by throwing aside brandy, unless we can procure the most *recherché* kinds, which are rich in ethers, and betaking ourselves to the use of the finest old port or sherry, or to some of the more excellent qualities of Rhenish or Hungarian wines. From six to twelve ounces per diem of fine old sherry . . . given in divided doses at intervals of half-an-hour, affords the ideal stimulant required under the circumstances; it is surprising how rapidly this treatment at the same time restores strength and regularity to the heart's action, and calms the nervous system, so as to allow of sweet and restorative sleep. . . . The physicians of the Westminster Hospital have had abundant opportunities of observing the effects in such circumstances of a very splendid old sherry, of which the late Duke of Northumberland presented a large quantity to the hospital; and for our own part we are convinced that the influence of such a liquor is something entirely distinct from that of its mere alcohol.

Other acute conditions, including delirium, cardiac ex-

haustion, catarrhal inflammations, influenza, acute neu-
roses, and neuralgia, were discussed at length, with recommended dosages of various unmedicated and medicated
wines, drugs, and diet. Dr. Anstie opposed any use of
alcohol in tetanus, delirium tremens or "catarrhal inflammation of the stomach." In chronic complaints, he
favored burgundy for dyspepsia, port for "simple anemia," and port wine and stout for anorexia, but doubted
the advisability of any alcoholic beverage in cases of
chronic mucous discharges. He acknowledged the contemporary medical view that "alcohol was murder in
phthisis," but expressed his belief that there were some
cases in which very light wines, "free from acetous decomposition," might be useful.

Dr. Anstie's views were echoed thirty years later by
Dr. Yorke-Davies, a member of the Royal College of
Surgeons, in a work entitled *Wine and Health—How to
Enjoy Both*.[19] Dr. Yorke-Davies recommended "pure
dry claret, hock, and moselle" as "suitable for the diabetic," but prohibited sweet wines, beer, and stout in
that disease. In cases of gastric acidity he permitted "good
Californian white wines, Australian white wines, Hungarian wines, and the wines of many other countries," as
well as cognac and old whisky. For anemia, he specified
"those wines containing iron, such as burgundy or St.
Raphael," stating that although the general opinion favored stout, burgundy, port, and sherry for this condition, they were not absolutely necessary. He also included
wine and spirits in the diets of his gouty patients, but
stated that "sweet wines, beer, and new cider should not
be touched." Dr. Yorke-Davies devoted much of his

book to warnings against alcoholic excesses, especially by the military, and to his opposition against spirits, strong wines, and the "doctored" wines of Cette, Marseilles, and Bordeaux.

In continental Europe, where intemperance was considerably less of a problem than in England, physicians were not compelled to defend their use of wine, and their artful prescriptions were amply recorded in the medical literature. Typical of the extensive works were the *Traité sur l'Usage et les Effets des Vins* of Loebenstein-Loebel (1817), the *Clinique Médicale de l'Hôtel Dieu* of Armand Trousseau (1861), the *Traité de Médecine* of Jean-Martin Charcot (1825-1893), and the *Valor Terapeutico del Vino de Jerez* of Alexandre and Aparici (1903).

Loebenstein-Loebel, a physician of Strasbourg, administered wines by spoonful, goblet, and enema for a seemingly endless list of ailments. In his voluminous text, wherever he prohibited one particular wine for one therapeutic purpose, he recommended another wine in its place; where rhine wine might fail to effect a particular cure, he specified barsac, malaga, or port; if tokay essence proved inefficacious, he substituted champagne, Würzburger, or French or Turkish *vins généreux*.[20]

Trousseau, a professor of the Paris faculty and physician at the *Hôtel Dieu*, devised a famous "most powerful hydragogue" composed of white wine, juniper berries, squill, digitalis, and potassium acetate. He asserted that "this wine, which I have used for a number of years, and my colleagues have accepted the formula, is easily tolerated and apparently cures symptoms of heart disease in a great number of cases." Trousseau also recorded "remarkable results" from his use of sherry, madeira, and malaga in chlorosis, of old red *vin ordinaire* during convalescence after typhoid fever, and of wine in small quantities for dyspepsia. In gout, he wrote that "when wine is not harmful to the individual, Spanish wines are preferable to French or Rhine wines."[21]

The *Traité de Médecine* of Charcot, the celebrated French neurologist and physician to the Salpêtrière, was an encyclopedia of the treatments found useful by the leading European clinicians of his time. Wine, usually well diluted with water and in some cases with a few drops of cognac added, was specified in pernicious anemia, in diets for aneurism of the aorta, as a tonic in convalescence after diphtheria, in acute and severe eczemas, in scurvy, in broncho-pneumonia as a complication of measles in children, in hemorrhagic measles, and in various programs for obesity. Generous wines were prescribed in fractionated doses in stomatitis and in advanced stages of endocarditis. Wine was prohibited in cancer of the stomach, in chronic enteritis, and chronic arteriosclerosis. In pulmonary tuberculosis, Charcot prohibited wine as a "habitual" drink, but nevertheless permitted a glass of claret or of *vin généreux* at the end of a meal.[22]

Typical of the medical claims made for individual wines in the countries of their origin were the writings of Alexandre and Aparici concerning sherry. This wine, they asserted, "given in moderate doses, in 24 hours up to 500 gr according to how much the person can tolerate . . . is necessary for persons to reestablish lost

energy, restore the powers of individuals of feeble constitution, of convalescents from grave diseases, for the over-
worked, and for the aged. . . . It is especially indicated
in pneumonia of old people. . . . It is a neurasthenic tonic
of immediate effect, stimulating the nervous system and
favoring oxidation."[23]

In the United States, the situation concerning wine in
medical practice resembled that in England. But England
had its Sandford, Druitt, Anstie, and Yorke-Davies, while
the American physicians prescribed wine but did not
write about it as medicine. Sir William Osler, the beloved
physician-in-chief of Johns Hopkins Hospital, and later
Regius Professor of Medicine at Oxford, rarely mentioned wine in any of his dozens of volumes and scientific
papers, but when asked for his views in 1917, said: "I
should be sorry to give up its use in the severe form of
enteric and pneumonic fevers."[24] Almost all published
American works which discussed the therapeutic use of
wine were either attacks on the medical profession by the
crusaders against alcohol, or books by lay writers on beverages, who quoted liberally the oral testimonials of their
doctor friends. Typical of the former was the favorite
text of the Women's Christian Temperance Union, by
Mrs. Martha Allen, entitled *Alcohol, a Dangerous and
Unnecessary Medicine—How and Why* (1900). On the
other hand, a favorable view was presented in Thomas
McMullen's *Handbook of Wines* (New York, 1852),
in which a Doctor Sigmond was quoted as calling wine
"a fine stomachic which taken at its proper season invig-
orates the mind and body" and a Professor Brande was
credited with the statement that sherry is "a fine whole-

some wine, and when of due age and good condition, free from excess of acid matter, is a valuable article of the materia medica."

Thus, during the latter years of the nineteenth century, wine was still a universal medicine, prescribed in the dietary of the healthy and in the treatment of the whole spectrum of human complaints, with few contraindications to its use. Physicians knew the values of wine by close observations of the patients to whom it was administered. But the authorities who had established its uses, in the literature of medicine, were all dead—Hippocrates and Galen, Avicenna and Maimonides, Nicholas and Arnald, Theodoric and Bruno, Anstie and Yorke-Davies.

By 1900, new medicines were appearing: aspirin, the alleviant of pain and fever, soon followed by the barbitals, which produced sedation; by the vitamins, which relieved deficiency diseases and then became a fetish; by the hormones, potent and dangerous; by the numerous sulfa drugs, which later faded; by the antibiotics, which paralyzed bacteria; by the tranquilizers; and by the swelling stream of newly-developed synthetics and purported specifics, each crowding its predecessors into obsolescence. Each new product was accompanied by a deluge of elaborately designed laboratory and clinical data attesting dramatically to its marvelous efficacy.

For wine, such proofs, by measurable criteria, were generally lacking. The only conclusive evidence of its value was the test of centuries—as a harmless stomachic, diuretic, and sedative, gently beneficial in virtually all ailments, in all segments of the population, uniformly effective despite the biologic variations which so frequently nullify, and often violently repulse, treatment by modern drugs.

While things new captured medical interest, the old fell into disuse. Ancient healing in general came under professional and popular scorn, and volumes purporting to expose medieval and folk medicine became national best-sellers. A whole generation of physicians entered practice without knowledge of the time-tested remedies safely employed by their predecessors. And wine, besmirched by the prohibitionists, erased from the pharmacopoeia despite its magnificent record as a therapeutic agent, was gradually dismissed from most medical practice.

BIBLIOGRAPHY

1. Druitt, Robert: *Report on the Cheap Wines from France, Germany, Italy, Austria, Greece, Hungary, and Australia—Their Use in Diet and Medicine.* London, Henry Renshaw, 1873, p. 110.

2. Pavy, F. W.: *Treatise on Food and Dietetics.* New York, William Wood & Co., 2nd ed., 1881, pp. 368 ff.

3. Guthrie: *A History of Medicine, op. cit.,* p. 207.

4. *The Juice of the Grape—or Wine Preferable to Water.* By a Fellow of the Colleges. Printed for W. Lewis, under Tom's Coffee-House, Covent Garden, London, 1824, pp. 10, 16, 38.

5. Heberden, William: *An Introduction to the Study of Physic,* with Prefatory Essay by Leroy Crummer. New York, Paul B. Hoeber, Inc., 1929, pp. 22, 156-157.

6. Sandford, William: *A Few Practical Remarks on the Medicinal Effects of Wine and Spirits.* London, J. Tymbs, 1799, pp. iv, v, 8-9, 20.

7. *Ibid.:* p. 27.

8. Henderson, Alexander: *The History of Ancient and Modern Wines.* London, Baldwin, Cradock and Joy, 1824, pp. 346-348.

9. *Ibid.:* p. 349.

10. *Ibid.:* pp. 355-356.

11. *Ibid.:* p. 353.

12. Carpenter, William M.: *On the Use and Abuse of Alcoholic Liquors in Health and Disease.* London, Charles Gilpin, 1851, p. 249.

13. Tovey, Charles: *Wine and Wine Countries*. London, Hamilton, Adams & Co., 1862, p. 287.

14. Druitt: *op. cit.,* pp. 2, 174.

15. Samuelson, James, of the Middle Temple, Barrister-at-Law: *The History of Drink*. London, Trübner & Co., 1878, p. 231.

16. *Loc. cit.*

17. *Ibid.:* p. 233.

18. Anstie, Francis E.: *On the Uses of Wine in Health and Disease.* London, Macmillan and Co., 1877.

19. Yorke-Davies, N. E.: *Wine and Health—How to Enjoy Both.* London, Chatto & Windus, 1909, pp. 74, 92-96.

20. Loebenstein-Loebel, E.: *Traité sur l'Usage et les Effets des Vins.* Strasbourg, Levrault, 1817.

21. Trousseau, A.: *Clinique Médicale de l'Hôtel Dieu.* Paris, Baillère, 1913, Vol. 2, p. 37, Vol. 3, p. 391.

22. Charcot, J. M.: *Traité de Médecine.* Paris, Masson, 1899-1905, 10 vols.

23. Alexandre and Aparici: Valor terapeutico del vino de Jerez. *Int. Med. Congr.,* 14th, Madrid, C. R. Sec. Thérap., p. 435 (1903).

24. Quoted by E. H. Williams in Alcohol and therapeutics. *Med. Rec., 92:* 666-668 (1917).

14

The Demonstration of the Physiologic Effects of Wine

A RENAISSANCE IN SCIENCE occurred in the mid-nineteenth century. Men sought logical explanations for physical phenomena, and replaced folklore with facts in many areas of knowledge. Key to this development was the introduction of the experimental method, a forward step usually identified with the great French physiologist, Claude Bernard. For Claude Bernard was the first to induce disease artificially for experimental purposes, and to his systematic research is credited much of our present knowledge of the physiology of the digestive, nervous, and endocrine systems. The experimental method made it possible to test and measure the physiologic effects of medicinal substances, instead of accepting the testimony of empirical observations as physicians had done for many centuries.

Among the substances subjected early to scientific study was alcohol, and it was Claude Bernard himself who, in 1857, in his private laboratory on the left bank of the Seine, first measured its effect on gastric digestion in animals, observing that in concentrated form it retarded the digestive process. In these experiments Bernard used only pure alcohol.[1] Although he was the son of a wine producer, there is no record that he ever studied wine.

Contemporary with Claude Bernard was Louis Pasteur, who explored alcoholic fermentation and established the foundations of bacteriology. Pasteur was a staunch advocate of wine, and his description of it as "the most healthful, the most hygienic of beverages"[2] has been widely quoted, although his extensive studies of wine, which impressed him with the need to protect its soundness as a public health measure, never included any actual experiments with it as a medicine.

The first recorded scientific attempt at an objective comparison of the physiologic effects of wine with those of alcohol was a pioneering experiment by Edmund A. Parkes, the founder of army medical hygiene in England, and his co-worker, the Polish count, Cyprian Wollowicz. About 1870, at the Army Medical College in London, these gentlemen measured the heart action, body temperature, and excretions of a soldier to whom they administered water and red Bordeaux wine in varying doses at mealtimes during three successive ten-day periods. Their experiment ended in an impasse. While the subject affirmed that the wine agreed with him better than alcohol, there was nothing in the tabulated results to confirm this. Parkes and Wollowicz admitted that "the influence of the sugar, of the salts, and of the acidity must be appreciated by other methods," that the complexities of wine and their subjective evaluation were too many to permit of simple measurement.[3]

There were scores of early experiments with ethyl alcohol, with findings which in the main have been confirmed by subsequent research. In Germany in 1877, Carl Binz demonstrated that alcohol is utilized in the body;[4] Emil Kraepelin (1899) studied its effects on the motor functions of the brain;[5] and R. O. Neumann (1901) established that 95 per cent of the potential energy of alcohol is readily available for immediate use.[6] In Russia, Kuwschinski (1888) demonstrated that the flow of pancreatic juice in dogs is increased after the administration of alcohol.[7] In France, Rabuteau (1870) initiated the first comprehensive toxicity studies on alcohol,[8, 9] which were amplified later by Joffroy (1895);[10] while Gréhant and Nicloux (1899) determined the rate at which alcohol is metabolized,[11] and Emile Duclaux (1902) confirmed the findings of Binz.[12] In the United States, some of the first scientific investigations were performed by Warren Lombard (1892) at Clark University. He found that alcohol in small quantities produces brief increases in muscular output, but although Lombard conducted his tests with both claret and whisky, he failed to compare the effects of the wine with those of the whisky.[13]

Apparently most of these research workers assumed that all alcoholic beverages produce the same physiologic effects, varying only according to the degree of concentration—that alcohol is the only active constituent. This assumption was first effectively challenged when the pupils of Binz, at the Institute of Pharmacology in Bonn, measured the effects on respiratory volume of human and animal subjects to whom they administered, orally, varying doses of wine, brandy, and solutions of pure alcohol. The conclusions were published by Krautwig (1893) and Vogel (1897)[14] and were corroborated by the experiments of Wendelstadt (1899). To both fatigued and non-fatigued human subjects, Wendelstadt administered sherry, rhine wine, champagne, cognac, and alcohol, making the latter palatable by the addition of sugar and lemon juice. He found that both the aromatic wines and the brandy produced markedly greater increases in expired air than did identical concentrations of alcohol, and that the effect was most pronounced in conditions of bodily weariness.[15] In reviewing this work some years afterward, John J. Abel, the Johns Hopkins pharmacologist and editor of the *Journal of Pharmacology and Therapeutics*, commented that the findings supported the observations made by clinicians, namely, "that the highly flavored wines are better respiratory stimulants than the plainer sorts."[16]

The many epidemics of cholera in Europe following the Franco-Prussian War, and the discovery by Robert Koch that the disease is transmitted by drinking-water, stimulated a widespread search for preventive measures. Professor Alois Pick, at the Vienna Institute of Hygiene, undertook to test the popular belief that by adding wine, water could be made safe to drink. This prophylactic measure can be traced back twenty-five centuries to Cyrus the Great, who ordered his armies to carry wine on the march to Babylonia as a protection until they could become accustomed to the local waters.[17] Professor Pick exposed the bacilli of cholera and typhoid to various mixtures of wine and water, and found that the bacteria were soon destroyed. The more wine he added, the quicker was the effect. He announced these results during the cholera epidemic of Hamburg in 1892, stating that wine should be added to water, but well in advance of drinking.[18] Similar tests were subsequently made by Jean-Emile Sabrazès and André Marcandier at the Pasteur Institute in 1907; and the French public was advised that to be on the safe side, white wine should be added to water six hours before meals and that for red wine the interval should be twelve hours.[19]

Thirty years later, Remlinger and Bailly in France, using ordinary Algerian wines, both red and white, obtained comparable results on four strains of dysentery bacilli, but noted that the bactericidal effect varied with the type of wine and with the kind of microorganism. They suggested that the antibacterial power might be due in part to the tannins in wine, although this seemed to be contradicted by their finding that red wines, which are richest in tannin, were slightly less active than the white.[20] Clearly, the active agent was something other than alcohol, because it has been repeatedly shown that aqueous solutions of plain alcohol have no effect against most bacilli until the alcoholic strength is increased well above 30 per cent, nearly three times the concentration of natural wine.[21]

During World War II, enteric diseases, spread by contaminated water, presented an important medical problem in the Mediterranean theater. John Gardner, an American pharmacy student engaged in military field sanitation, noticed that the local populace, who followed the ancient custom of adding wine to water for drinking, seemed to be free of these disorders. This gave Gardner an idea. He knew that in most military campaigns through the centuries, deaths from typhoid fever, cholera, and bacillary dysentery far outnumbered battle casualties. He reasoned, however, that this could not have been true of the early Greek and Roman campaigns, when those empires flourished and their armies succeeded in conquering the lands surrounding the Mediterranean. Were their military successes made possible, he wondered, by the addition of wine to drinking water? After the war, and upon resuming his studies at the University of California, Gardner began a series of experiments with wine, using four species of bacteria. He readily found that red wines possess antibacterial activity which could not be ascribed to their content of alcohol, aldehydes, tannins, or acids. A curious feature of his results was the observation that when *Staphylococcus aureus* and *Escherichia coli* were exposed to newly-fermented red wine, the growth-inhibiting power increased as the wine was diluted with distilled water from a concentration of 1:10 to 1:100,000. Gardner then sought to identify the active fractions in the wine. He succeeded in isolating from dealcoholized red wine a compound, soluble in alcohol and in water, which completely inhibited the growth of *Staphylococ-*

cus aureus and *Bacillum megatherium*. Gardner described this compound as a "wine antibiotic," but was unable to identify it chemically.[22]

The antibiotic action observed by Gardner was subsequently traced by Jacques Masquelier and two of his doctoral students, Madame Hélène Jensen and Jean Lancepleine, at the University of Bordeaux, to the anthocyanins and related pigments of wine. In a series of reports beginning in 1953, they showed that some of these compounds, although inactive when extracted from grapes, developed bactericidal power following the fermentation of the grapes into wine.[23]

Scientists of other countries were slow in accepting the Bordeaux findings, largely because other investigators had tested plant anthocyanins for microbial activity and had found none. In 1959, at the University of Georgia, a team of workers headed by John J. Powers undertook an independent study, using anthocyanin fractions extracted from Pinot Noir wine, from bottled Concord grape juice, and from frozen strawberries, and testing them, apart from alcohol, on cultures of *Escherichia coli*, *Staphylococcus aureus*, and *Lactobacillus casei*. A year later the Powers group reported its findings: some of the fractions, primarily the colorless leuco-bases from wine, definitely inhibited the growth of the test organisms; other fractions, which might have retained traces of sugar, appeared to stimulate growth.[24, 25] By 1960, when the work of Powers and his associates was published, there no longer appeared to be any question that wine has antibacterial power independent of its alcoholic content.

After the pioneering work of Claude Bernard, scores

of investigators in Europe and America conducted studies of the effects of alcohol on the digestive system. Most of them assumed, as the majority of reviewers still assume today, that the actions of various alcoholic beverages differ only according to the concentration of alcohol, thereby ignoring the sharp differences between the effects of plain solutions of alcohol and the effects of wine.

So marked are these differences that when Wilhelm Buchner, at the Medical Clinic of Erlangen in Germany in 1881, made the first comparisons of the action of wine and beer with that of alcohol in the alimentary tract, his results seemed to explode the ancient reputation of fermented beverages as aids to digestion. Buchner, conducting experiments both *in vitro* and with human subjects, found that wines and malt beverages significantly retard the rate at which protein is digested, while alcohol in the same low concentrations does not.[26] Similar results were reported a decade later by Sir William Roberts in England. Roberts found, however, that while large quantities of wine, especially of sherry, retard proteolysis, small quantities of wine accelerate the process. He also demonstrated that dilute alcoholic solutions, including wines, stimulate the secretion of gastric juice and the muscular contractions of the stomach.[27]

Between 1893 and 1898, in extensive experiments on dogs at the Sheffield Laboratory of Physiological Chemistry at Yale University, the physiologists Russell Chittenden, Lafayette Mendel, and Holmes Jackson obtained results confirming the work of both Buchner and Roberts, and demonstrated that the differences in the effects of wines from those of alcohol are due principally to the extractives, the solid matter, contained in the wines. They found the inhibition of proteolysis produced by a California claret to be equivalent to that produced by an alcohol solution ten times as strong, while a white wine, with its lower content of solids, had far less retarding effect than the red. On the other hand, small amounts of claret added to gastric juice caused an appreciable increase in the rate of gastric digestion. The Yale physiologists demonstrated that alcoholic beverages in general stimulate the secretion of a concentrated gastric juice, both directly and indirectly through the influence of the alcohol absorbed from the intestine. They suggested that the inhibitory action of wine on proteolysis is neutralized by the increase in gastric flow.[28, 29] In summarizing the results of the Yale research, Chittenden expressed his full agreement with Sir William Roberts, that "a glass or two [of claret, hock, or sherry] with dinner or luncheon would evidently not produce any appreciable retardation of peptic action, but would . . . act as pure stimulants."[30]

Chittenden and his associates also investigated the effects of alcoholic beverages on salivary digestion, finding an inhibitory effect comparable to that on digestion in the stomach. Large amounts of wine caused retardation, while small amounts, their inhibiting action apparently overcome by the alkalinity of the saliva, caused no retardation.[31]

Many subsequent studies, such as those of Ludwig Kast (1906), Aksel Haneborg (1921), G. Franzen (1928), and Eric Ogden (1946), supported the principal findings of the Yale group. Kast, in experiments on dogs performed at the Institute of Pathology in Berlin, de-

termined that beverages containing up to 20 per cent alcohol promote both gastric secretion and stomach motility and indirectly increase the secretion of pancreatic
juice, and that solutions above 20 per cent are directly injurious. In stating his conclusions, Kast particularly recommended the consumption of wine with rich diets.[32]
Haneborg, working at the University of Christiania and
in the hospitals of that city, administered to 92 human
subjects test meals with ethyl alcohol, cognac, aquavit,
claret, rhine wine, and beers, and recovered through
esophageal tubes the contents of their stomachs. He
found that the wines and beers, unlike the diluted spirituous beverages, slowed proteolysis at first, and then by degrees, over a period of hours, gradually and markedly
increased it.[33] Franzen, at the Pharmacological Institute
of Jena, performed similar experiments on human subjects with sherry and found that their gastric secretions
increased markedly, while their stomach emptying times,
which were slowed by sherry administered at full
strength, were either unaffected or accelerated when the
sherry was diluted below 7 per cent.[34] Ogden, at the
University of California, tested eight normal male students in a similar fashion, comparing the effects of white
table wine and dealcoholized wine with a 14 per cent solution of alcohol, and confirmed the more sustained stimulation of gastric secretion which wine gives in contrast
to alcohol.[35]

More difficult to measure are the actions of these beverages on intestinal digestion, in which enzymes from the
intestinal secretions and the pancreas, and bile from the
liver, perform the major functions of transforming nu-

trients into forms that can be absorbed into the blood stream. Despite the complexities of experimentation in this area, several groups of investigators have succeeded in supplying pertinent data. In France, Maurice Loeper and associates administered wines by duodenal tube and by mouth to normal persons and to patients with liver disorders, and measured the resulting volumes of the bile and its content of nitrogen. Their results, reported in 1929, indicated that wines facilitate the assimilation of nitrogen and stimulate deamination by the liver; and furthermore, that sweet wines and white table wines are more active in this respect than red table wines.[36] In Italy, a research group headed by Emidio Serianni reported in 1955 on the excretion of hippuric acid by healthy young subjects and showed that red wine taken with meals accelerated the detoxification function of the liver, when compared with the ingestion of an aqueous alcoholic solution.[37] In California, John Carbone administered a liter of red table wine daily with diets controlled in calories and protein value to five chronic alcoholics suffering from severe liver cirrhosis, and found by liver biopsy that there was a marked clearing of the fatty and cellular infiltrations characteristic of this disease. The striking improvement shown by all five of his patients appeared to contradict the long-prevalent belief that an overly-liberal use of wine can itself cause cirrhosis.[38]

It has long been contended that a glass of wine taken with a meal high in fat content can alleviate the ensuing gastric distress and dyspepsia. That this is true in at least some cases of inability to absorb fatty foods—the malabsorption syndrome—was reported in 1960 by Theodore Althausen and associates at the University of California Gastrointestinal Research Laboratory. These workers administered wine to 24 patients who were unable to digest fat after having part of the stomach removed, an operation frequently performed for cancer or for complications of peptic ulcer. The ingestion of a dry white wine was shown to double fat absorption, as indicated by the amount of Vitamin A absorbed by these subjects. The rate of increased absorption varied from 35 to 431 per cent, averaging 125 per cent. At the same time, the patients demonstrated considerable clinical improvement. The malabsorption syndrome is believed to be due to an excess of the enzyme cholinesterase, which in turn causes inadequate secretion of pancreatic juice into the intestine. It also occurs in conditions not related to surgery, including tropical and non-tropical sprue, and in elderly patients.[39]

The psychic mechanism by which the whole digestive process is set in motion, and the relationship of appetite to efficient digestion, first began to receive attention through the work of Ivan Petrovich Pavlov, the Russian physiologist whose conditioned-reflex experiments on dogs laid the foundation for the science of psychodynamics. Pavlov termed alcohol "a psychic stomachicum," and in one of his lectures at St. Petersburg, published in 1910 in his work on the digestive glands, he related an instance of this from his own experience. After an illness in which he had completely lost his appetite, Pavlov sought to restore it by swallowing a mouthful of wine.

"I felt it quite distinctly pass along the oesophagus into my stomach," he said, "and literally at that moment perceived the onset of a keen appetite."[40]

At the Hull Physiological Laboratory of the University of Chicago, Anton Carlson explored the differences between hunger and appetite, and in the course of four years of study tested the belief that alcoholic beverages augment the sensation of hunger. He introduced dry and sweet wines, beer, diluted brandy, and a 10 per cent alcohol solution directly into the stomachs of human subjects, and measured the contractions of the stomach which accompany hunger. To his surprise, each of these fluids, instead of increasing the hunger contractions as he had expected, had the opposite effect, delaying the contractions for as long as two hours. Of all the drinks tested, the dry wines inhibited hunger contractions the most. In his book published in 1916, Carlson commented on "the singular condition of alcoholic beverages augmenting appetite and inhibiting hunger at the same time," and asked, "How are these results to be harmonized with the seeming stimulation of the appetite by alcoholic beverages taken by the mouth?"[41]

A partial explanation was contributed by Alan Winsor and E. I. Strongin in their experiments on salivary secretion, performed at Cornell University and reported in 1933. These workers offered the opinion that the sensation of appetite is caused by increases in the flow of saliva and digestive juices, which were observed to follow the administration of wine and other alcoholic beverages by mouth.[42]

But a fuller explanation, and one of paramount importance in the treatment of anorexia, was supplied by Franz Goetzl at the Permanente Foundation Institute of Medical Research in Oakland. Beginning in 1948, Goetzl and his co-workers conducted a series of studies on appetite, the intensity of which they measured by degrees of olfactory acuity, i.e., the ability of the subjects to detect various faint odors. Thereby these organoleptic tests were established on a sound physiologic basis. Upon finding in the early experiments that bitter tonics stimulate appetite and that sugar depresses it, Goetzl proceeded in 1950 to experiment with wines. His first tests showed that dry red wine, given with lunch, increases appetite and prevents both the postcibal decrease in olfactory acuity and the accompanying sensation of satiety. Goetzl then added sugar to the wine, repeated the experiment, and found that the appetites of his subjects were depressed. He next performed a control experiment with a 12.5 per cent solution of alcohol, equivalent to the strength of the wine, and determined that alcohol, like sugar, depresses appetite and produces satiety. In his later studies he confirmed that white wines are as effective as red, providing they are dry.

Seeking to identify the constituents which account for the appetite-stimulating effects of wine, Goetzl tested solutions of tannic, tartaric, and acetic acids, and with them obtained results similar to those produced by wine. He later undertook experiments with wine in the management of underweight. Thirty-six clinic patients suffering from lack of appetite were instructed to take 100 cc. of dry wine daily with lunch or dinner, and to keep daily records of their food intake. In periods of six to thirteen weeks, during which time the patients were seen and weighed weekly, the records showed increased daily caloric intake by all of them, from an average of 773 to an average of 1,228 calories daily. At the same time their body weights increased from an average of 94 pounds to an average of 109 pounds. Weight gains were observed in all but three of the subjects. Finally, Goetzl noticed not only an increased desire for food by his patients, but also a change in their food acceptance, that is, marked increases in their desire for proteins.[43, 44, 45, 46, 47]

During the same years, a seeming contradiction to the work of Goetzl was presented by the experiments of Giorgio Lolli and associates, which indicated the possible value of wine in the control of obesity. In 1952, these workers reported their analysis of the dietaries of Italians and Italo-Americans, in which they observed that the ingestion of quickly absorbable carbohydrates is appreciably lower among Italians, who regularly consume wine with meals, than among their counterparts in the United States, who have drifted away from the regular use of wine.[48] Following this, Lolli conducted an experiment with 35 obese patients in New York. They were placed on a diet including three to four ounces of dry table wine daily with the evening meal, alternating with a diet excluding wine. In most of the patients, the ingestion of wine was accompanied by a lowered daily caloric intake and by a gradual but consistent loss of body weight. The explanation offered by the Lolli group was that the alleviation of anxiety—the general tranquilizing effects of wine—counteracted the tendency to overeat, and in that manner produced the weight-reducing results.[49] Whether the relief of anxiety contributed also to the increased food intake of Goetzl's underweight patients remains a subject of speculation.

A different kind of investigation was undertaken in 1957 by Ephraim Engleman, director of the University of California Arthritis Clinical Study Center, in an effort to test the age-old belief that wine, especially port, is a cause of gout. Engleman and his co-workers conducted a nationwide study of the drinking histories of gout sufferers, enlisting the cooperation of university and government medical centers in Colorado, Michigan, and New York. They compiled the detailed drinking records and clinical histories of 200 male sufferers from classic gouty arthritis, and also of 269 male patients of matching socio-economic level who had non-gouty arthritis or other medical diseases, to serve as controls. The results showed that the intake of wine was lowest in the 200 patients with gout, that 61 per cent of them had used little or no wine during their lives, and that the men whose wine consumption index was the highest had never suffered from gout. Later, Engleman tested these statistical results clinically, by adding a daily ration of port wine, two glasses or more, to the diets of 20 gouty patients, continuing this in some of the cases for an entire year. In none of these was there any demonstrable effect upon the clinical course of the disease.[50]

Sixteen hundred years before the discovery of insulin, Aretaeus the Cappadocian, practicing medicine in Rome, described diabetes and used wine in its treatment,[51] as did countless other physicians through the subsequent centuries. The inclusion of alcoholic beverages in the diabetic diet was based entirely on clinical observations until 1906, when Benedict and Török, of the First Medical Clinic of Budapest, supplied the first conclusive evidence on the subject. These workers fed calculated diets to three diabetic and two normal subjects, and measured the sugar and ketone bodies eliminated in the urine. They next added fat to the meals, and then replaced the fat with alcohol of the same caloric value, in the form of cognac. All of the diabetic subjects showed markedly less glycosuria and a decided decrease in ketone excretion when the fat was replaced by the cognac. Similar results were obtained with wines and beers, with equally impressive evidence that these beverages accelerate the oxidation of carbohydrates. In their conclusion, these workers recommended that diabetic diets, except in cases of nephritis, should include rhine wine in quantities of a half liter to one liter daily, or dry champagne or "weak light beer." [52]

While Benedict and Török were working at Budapest, similar tests were being made in Munich by the pharmacologist Otto Neubauer. To four patients with diabetic acidosis and to three normal subjects he administered a carbohydrate-free diet, to which he added during two-day test periods, bread, bread with white wine (Kaiserstuhler), and the wine alone, varying the quantities of wine from .7 liter to 1.4 liters. On the days when wine was given, the patients with severe acidosis showed markedly lowered excretion of acetone bodies with concomitant decreases in glycosuria. The wine had less effect on sugar excretion among the diabetics without acidosis, although a decrease in acetonuria still occurred. There was no effect on the normal subjects. Neubauer interpreted these results to mean that the formation of acetone bodies was decreased by the action of the wine. His conclusion was that "the results certainly justify the use of moderate amounts of wine in cases of severe diabetic acidosis when no contraindication exists." [53]

Between 1918 and 1935, the studies of Burge[54] and of Soula and Baisset[55] established that small amounts of alcohol decrease blood sugar levels in diabetic patients. Then, at the Institute of Diet and Nutrition in Rome, Serianni and his associates demonstrated in experiments published in 1937 that alcohol has the same effect when administered in the form of wine. These workers reported, further, that the ingestion of grapes seemed to act favorably on the metabolism of carbohydrates in diabetes.[56] In the following year they showed that the ingestion of wine with a meal produces a lower sugar level in the blood of the veins than in the capillary blood vessels, whereas alcohol has no such effect. Serianni suggested that there is present in the grape a substance possessing an action on carbohydrate metabolism similar to that of insulin.[57]

A simpler explanation than that offered by Serianni was provided in 1952 by Jacob Weinstein and Joseph Roe, of the George Washington University School of Medicine. These workers compared the rates at which different sugars, injected intravenously, are removed from the blood stream of animals and hospital patients. Their results showed that fructose is utilized more rapidly than glucose. Since the sugar present in wine is chiefly levulose, or *d*-fructose, the conclusion of Weinstein and

Roe that "fructose may prove to be a valuable carbohydrate in the management of the diabetic patient, and in the treatment of the patient with low glycogen reserves"[58] has special significance referable to wine.

That the regular use of wine with meals may play a part in preventing diabetes was suggested in the survey of the dietaries and drinking habits of nearly 500 Italian and Italo-American adults, reported in 1953 by Lolli, Serianni, and their colleagues. As part of the routine studies included in the project, glucose tolerance tests were performed in 476 of the subjects, with the unexpected result that 15 obviously diabetic glucose tolerance curves and 58 borderline reactors were disclosed. Examination of the dietary records showed that most of these borderline or true diabetic subjects either drank no alcoholic beverage, or consumed only very small quantities. The glucose tolerance curves in all of the other subjects, most of whom were regular users of wine, were found to be normal.[59]

Following the recent introduction of orally effective blood-sugar-reducing agents, the Italian group made a study to determine the effects of wine administered in conjunction with these drugs. To the diets of 30 male diabetics, of whom ten were on insulin, ten on one of the new hypoglycemic agents, and ten under dietary control only, there were added sizable quantities of carbohydrates and a daily ration of wine. In all three groups, no untoward rises in blood sugar levels were observed. "From this investigation," said Claudia Balboni, one of the investigators, "it appears that wine can be safely and usefully included in the diet of very large segments of the diabetic population, not only because this regimen seems to be harmless, but also because it may contribute significantly to adequate control of carbohydrate metabolism." [60]

It was Hippocrates who, four centuries before the birth of Christ, first observed that "thin wines pass better by urine" and that dark and harsh wines are "more dry . . . consuming the moisture out of the body." [61] Experimental support for these statements was supplied in 1911 by Pierre-Paulin Carles, the director of chemical and pharmaceutical research at the medical school of Bordeaux. Carles found white wines decidedly more effective as diuretics than red wines, but was unable to explain the reason. [62] Actually, both red and white wines supply potassium bitartrate, an effective diuretic, and the greater efficiency of the white wines has not yet been explained.

The usefulness of wine in the treatment of kidney disease, both to stimulate diuresis and to brighten an otherwise monotonous and unappealing diet, has long been known to clinicians, but food technologists at the University of California have demonstrated other values in addition. In 1931, upon observing that the ash of grapes, of grape juice, and of grape concentrate is decidedly alkaline, Lawrence G. Saywell, in the university's Fruit Products Laboratory, undertook an investigation to determine whether these substances might be of value in the diet for the purpose of maintaining the alkaline reserve. Sixteen male subjects ingested these grape products together with basic diets, and their urinary excretions were studied. The results showed increases in the urinary pH, decreases in the excretion of ammonia, corresponding decreases in the total acidity, and increases in the alkaline reserve above the normal for each subject. Approximately 94 per cent of the ingested organic acids appeared to be oxidized.[63] A further study, using white and red table wine, was undertaken in the same laboratory by Julius Fessler, Emil Mrak, William Cruess, and J. J. Hayes, with similar results, showing that the presence of the natural buffering agents in wine prevents the acidosis which normally is produced by alcohol itself.[64]

Many of the modern findings concerning the physiologic effects of wine are given additional meaning by the results of a more fundamental kind of investigation— the identification of the complex chemical constituents of this simple beverage. The principal acids, salts, and mineral components had already been identified by 1854, when Professor G. J. Mulder of the University of Utrecht wrote his comprehensive work on *The Chemistry of Wine*.[65] Since Mulder's time, more than one hundred additional compounds have been identified in grapes, musts, and in old and new wines. Many of these have been demonstrated to possess important pharmacologic properties. Reference has already been made to the anthocyanins, about a dozen of which have been identified; to the sugars, levulose and *d*-glucose; to the tannins, which include a number of related substances; and to the alcohols, which are represented not only by ethanol but also by a whole series of higher alcohols. Entirely new areas of research were opened during the present century by such modern procedures as high vacuum distillation and chromatography, and, between the years 1949 and 1961, these technics made it possible to identify numerous previously unknown volatile and non-volatile substances in grapes and wines.

As early as 1880, Carles, then beginning his work in Bordeaux, demonstrated by simple analytic techniques that there are measurable amounts of iron in all types of wine[66]—a fact which gained significance half a century later, when George Marsh and K. Nobusada, at the University of California, found that approximately 80 per cent of the iron present in wine is in the reduced or ferrous form, and is thus physiologically available.[67] (Wines usually contain 5 to 20 mg. of iron per liter.[68]) This availability may well explain why wine has long been found useful in the mild anemias which result from iron-deficient diets.

These and other findings have directed attention to the possible physiologic values of the other inorganic components of wines. In 1957, Lucia and Hunt demonstrated, by analyzing 277 samples of wine for sodium and potassium, that potassium greatly exceeds sodium, and that most wines are therefore desirable additions to the relatively flat low-sodium diets of hypertensive and cardiac patients. The averages, expressed in mg. per 100 cc., were 5.44 sodium and 82.90 potassium for white table wines, 5.56 and 104.23 for red table wines, and 7.10 and 89.65 for dessert wines.[69] The study of Gottlieb et al.[70] in 1959 on the influence of alcohol and dietary magnesium on hypercholesterolemia and atherogenesis in the rat led to the speculation that magnesium, which occurs in amounts of 60 to 144 mg. per liter in normal wines,[71] may be of importance to the cardiovascular system. Interest was also expressed in the calcium content of natural wines, which varies from 50 to 200 mg. per liter.[72] This may have supplemental nutritional value, especially since the daily calcium requirement of adults may be as low as 200 mg.[73]

In 1928, the French nutritionist, Lucie Randoin, working under the auspices of the Ministry of Agriculture in France, demonstrated for the first time that vitamin C and the vitamins of the B complex are present in wines.[74, 75] Subsequent investigations by Agnes Fay Morgan and co-workers[76, 77, 78] and J. G. B. Castor[79] in California, and by Henri Flavier,[80] Relda Cailleau and Louis Chevillard,[81] Jean Ribéreau-Gayon,[82] Emile Peynaud,[83] and others in France, established that while much of the antiscorbutic vitamin is lost in vinification, certain of the B vitamins are preserved in nutritionally important amounts.

Of particular interest are the findings from these experiments that wines retain sufficient quantities of thiamin, riboflavin, pantothenic acid (the growth-stimulating vitamin), pyridoxin, niacin, and folic acid (the anti-anemia vitamin) to add appreciably to the daily vitamin intake. Certain wines, primarily the sweet red types, were shown by Morgan and associates to contain 71 per cent more riboflavin and 45 per cent more folic acid than do the grape juices from which the wines were made.[84] Evidently the yeast releases additional amounts of these vitamins during fermentation. In general, these nutrients were found to survive best in the sweet red wines of the port type, thus partially supporting the ancient belief in their blood-building quality. On the other hand, the dry red and white wines showed higher amounts of pantothenic acid. Young wines and those subjected to a minimum of treatment in the winery were highest in their content of natural vitamins, most of which, however, are readily destroyed when exposed to sunlight.

The polyphenols and tannins of grapes have been studied by French,[85, 86] American, and Russian investigators interested in those plant substances, such as rutin, which are thought to promote the resistance of the capillaries to hemorrhage and to have other important effects on homeostasis. The substances which produce such effects are said to possess "vitamin P properties," although "vitamin P" is not a single definite chemical entity, as are the true vitamins. In 1949, Floyd DeEds, in the pharmacologic laboratory of the government research station at Albany, California, reported the isolation from grapes and grape residue of a compound possessing "vitamin P properties." In experiments on animals, the grape substance was found to retard the rate of oxidation of epinephrine and ascorbic acid, to prolong the relaxation of intestinal smooth muscle, and to reduce the injury from experimentally produced frostbite.[87] Subsequently, the Russian scientist Durmishidze, working with both grapes and wines, stressed the relationship of the tannins, such as *d*-catechol and *l*-gallocatechol, to the capillary-strengthening action.[88, 89] If future work were to establish that grapes possess this quality in important degree, it would confirm the empirical observations of the Spanish court physician who prescribed a diet of grapes and wine for the Prince of Asturias, the first recorded haemophiliac member of the royal family of Spain.[90]

That much remains to be learned about the nutritive and protective components of wine is emphasized by an experiment conducted in 1952 by Michel Flanzy and Jean Causeret at the National Institute of Agronomic Research in France. To three groups of young rats they gave high but not acutely intoxicating doses of alcohol, of red wine, and of brandy distilled from the same wine, administering all of the beverages at a 12.5 per cent alcohol concentration. A fourth, or control, group received no alcohol. After two months, the rats were sacrificed. It was found that only the animals which received wine were similar in growth and organ composition to the control rats which had received no alcohol.[91]

The complex chemical composition of wine also accounts for its widespread employment in modern pharmacy. The reasons usually given for its use, in preference to alcohol, as a menstruum for medication, are its mild acidity and its buffering action. These values were demonstrated in experiments by Louis Greengard at St. Louis in 1940, when he showed that vitamin B_1, when prepared in aqueous alcohol solutions, readily precipitates as thiochrome and becomes physiologically ineffective, but that the vitamin is stable when dissolved in detannated white wine.[92] Still other values, as yet unexplained, were found by the neurologist Howard Fabing in his comparisons of wine and alcohol as extractives of the belladonna alkaloid for the treatment of Parkinson's disease. In his experiments at the University of Cincinnati, Fabing prepared two extracts of the alkaloid, one using white wine and the other a 12 per cent solution of ethyl alcohol, and administered both to animals. The wine extractive successfully produced the neurotranquilizing effects which relieve the muscular rigidity and uncontrollable tremors of the disease. The alcohol preparation produced delirium and other unmistakable signs of toxicity.[93]

Early in the present century, Oswald Loeb in Germany (1905) demonstrated that perfusates containing minor amounts of alcohol (0.13 to 0.3 per cent) produce a noticeable stimulating effect on the isolated mammalian heart.[94] Later investigators conducted similar experiments, with the further finding that with concentrations more than 1.0 per cent, the action of the heart is materially weakened.[95]

In the pharmacologic laboratory of Novorossiisk University at Odessa during World War I, it occurred to a Russian research worker, Ivan Gregorivich Koutateladze, that this method offered a way to determine whether wine deserves its ancient reputation as a cardiac restorative and vasodilator—whether wine might have an action different from that of its alcohol. He conducted a series of experiments on the isolated heart of a cat, using a Bessarabian white table wine. In his first tests, he compared the effect of the wine, diluted to 0.1 per cent alcoholic strength, with that of an equivalent solution of ethanol. The alcohol at first depressed the heart action, while the wine produced stimulation; and later, when the stimulating effect of the alcohol became apparent, the wine produced even greater activity. Koutateladze then began a search among the components of wine for the substance responsible for the stimulation. Eventually, by distilling off the wine, he obtained a brownish, bitter-sweet residue, soluble in both absolute alcohol and water—a product of fermentation, since it was not found in the original grape juice. In dilutions of 1:500,000, this substance, without alcohol, increased the coronary blood flow and doubled the output of the heart. Koutateladze classified the substance chemically as an amine, and compared its initial action to that of digitalin. He reported his work at a medical meeting in Odessa in 1916. When it was published in a Russian journal in 1919,[96] at the height of the Bolshevist upheaval, it escaped the notice of most European and American investigators.

Nearly forty years after Koutateladze, separate investigations by pharmacologists in Finland and California attracted widespread notice. Their key findings confirmed the Russian discovery that nonalcoholic substances obtained from wines produce markedly stimulating cardiovascular effects. At the University of Helsinki, Osmo Vartiainen reported that a grape brandy with rich aroma increased coronary blood flow in the isolated rabbit heart by 10 to 25 per cent, whereas ethyl alcohol had only a very slight effect.[97] In the Department of Pharmacology and Experimental Therapeutics of the University of California, Carlo Romano, Frederick Meyers, and Hamilton Anderson tested aliphatic aldehydes and other compounds isolated from zinfandel wine on dogs and cats, and on the isolated tissues. They found that the volatile component propionaldehyde, in particular, has a pronounced stimulating effect on blood pressure and in other respects is pharmacologically similar to the body's own pressure-maintaining substance—norepinephrine or arterenol.[98]

In 1957, Morgan and her co-workers in California reported the results of experiments with laboratory animals on the utilization of calories from alcohol and from wines, and the specific effects on cholesterol metabolism. Young rats and hamsters were fed normal and cholesterol-rich diets with: (a) water, (b) a 15 per cent alcohol solution, and (c) dry red and dry white wines of 15 per cent alcoholic content. In comparison with the water- and alcohol-fed groups, and with total fluid intake held constant, the wine-fed animals were found to have significantly lower liver fat levels and as much as 50 per cent lower cholesterol levels in the blood, livers, and adrenals. In the same report, Dr. Morgan suggested that the role of tension in affecting the cholesterol level may be reflected in the fact that serum cholesterol content was highest in the animals whose water intake was restricted, and that water deprivation may have acted as a stress factor for these animals.[99]

It had already been shown by Campbell Moses[100] that certain plant polyphenols lower the formation of blood cholesterol in animals. Such effects have been demonstrated with a flavonoid found in oranges, with a polyphenol isolated from artichokes, and with quercetol, which is found in many plants. Leucocyanidol, one of the leucoanthocyanins identified in wine,[101] has been shown to precipitate lipoproteins in the blood serum.[102] The publication of Dr. Morgan's work with wine was followed by the report of Masquelier, who demonstrated with chromatographic measurements that a number of polyphenols capable of reducing the cholesterol level in animals are present in red wines.[103]

While more data are required to justify a conclusion concerning arterial disease in man, a 1961 investigation in Italy lends some clinical support to the widely-held Italian medical opinion that the regular use of wine in the diet may have a preventive effect on arterial degenerative diseases. Seventy-two men and eight women convalescing from cardiac attacks were studied to ascertain their eating and drinking habits during the years, months, and days prior to the attacks. It was learned that 13 were abstainers, 32 had been using less than 500 cc. of wine daily, 27 had used 500 to 1,000 cc., and only 8 had used 1,000 cc. or more. Of further interest was the finding that 25 of the patients had significantly decreased their wine intake shortly before the myocardial infarction—in 18 cases six months before, and in seven cases within a week before the attacks.[104]

Apparently it was the Parisian, Nestor Gréhant, working in the Laboratory of General Physiology, who in 1899 first related blood alcohol levels to the intoxicating effects of alcoholic beverages. By administering a 10 per cent alcohol solution to dogs through an esophageal tube, he discovered the relationships between dosage, body weight, and the level of alcohol in the blood. He recorded his results in graphs which portrayed the blood alcohol curves and demonstrated the rate at which ethanol is absorbed into the blood stream and the rate at which it is oxidized and excreted from the body.[105] Gréhant's experiments opened an entire field of alcohol research, in which some of the most significant differences between the effects of wine and of other beverages were clearly demonstrated by others.

During the first World War, Sir Edward Mellanby, conducting investigations by government request at London University to guide wartime controls of the sale of liquor, made the first comparisons between the intoxicating effects of dilute and concentrated alcohol solutions and between fermented and distilled beverages. Mellanby was the first to show that earlier and higher blood alcohol peaks were produced by the stronger beverages than by the weaker, and by whisky diluted to the strength of stout, than by stout at normal strength. He also compared the effects of alcohol administered in water with those of alcohol administered in milk, and the effects when alcohol was taken with bread, cheese, or fat, observing the lower and later peak blood levels produced when alcohol was taken with these other foodstuffs. He was the first to proclaim that "milk is the most effective foodstuff for delaying the absorption of alcohol into the blood." Although Mellanby's principal experiments were performed with dogs, he later repeated them on human subjects, and reported that while man is more sensitive to alcohol than the dog is, the results were otherwise comparable.[106]

In 1941, at the Yale Laboratory of Applied Physiology, Howard Haggard and co-workers confirmed that the alcohol in beer is absorbed more slowly than are equivalent doses of alcohol in the form of whisky or gin. Their results also indicated that the blood alcohol curve returns to the baseline in approximately the same period of time after administration of equivalent amounts of alcohol in each of these beverages, thus indicating an equal rate of oxidation and elimination.[107]

It remained for Henry W. Newman, the late Stanford neurologist, to show that the alcohol of wine is assimilated much more slowly than alcohol is in comparable aqueous solutions, and that a more moderate and prolonged elevation in the blood alcohol level results, without the high and brief peaks caused by spirituous beverages. Newman administered alcohol, whisky, gin, and port and burgundy wines, all at 13 per cent alcoholic strength, to two fasting human subjects, and found markedly slower absorption and lower peaks in blood alcohol from the wines than from the other beverages. He then administered a comparable dose of alcohol, adjusted to the same pH and buffer capacity as the port wine, and obtained approximately the same blood alcohol curve as with the port. This caused him to conclude that the slower absorption of alcohol from wine is ascribable to the buffer capacity of the wine.[108, 109]

Subsequently, Serianni and his colleagues, conducting blood alcohol researches at the Institute of Diet and Nutrition in Rome, measured the physiologic and psychologic effects of divided doses of wine and of solutions of alcohol with and without meals, thus more nearly duplicating real life situations. Serianni found evidence of radical differences that could be attributed only to the non-alcoholic components of wine, and suggested that there is an increase in the rate of oxidation of the alcohol contained in wine, probably resulting from a general stimulation of liver function.[110]

The demonstrations that wine is less intoxicating than

equivalent solutions of alcohol have recently developed intensified scientific interest in the view expressed by Thomas Jefferson and many others that the regular use of wine is a preventive of alcoholism. One study supporting this thesis has already been mentioned, the four-year survey in which Lolli and others compared the diets, parental attitudes toward alcohol, and the drinking patterns of Italians in Italy and of Italian immigrants and their descendants in the United States.[111, 112, 113, 114]

After 1953, several teams of research workers began further investigations to determine the extent to which the conclusions of Lolli and his co-workers are true. Studies of the drinking histories of alcoholics were made in California, New York, Brazil, France, Switzerland, and Sweden. In each location, interviews were conducted with alcoholics to ascertain their earliest drinking experiences, the beverages involved, and their choice of beverages during episodes of intoxication. From the massive data assembled, the conclusions were readily evident: alcoholism is rare when wine is customarily used with meals, and especially where it is introduced as a food in family surroundings relatively early in childhood.[115, 116, 117, 118]

With relatively few exceptions, the broadened alcohol research studies during the present century have emphasized only the excessive use and the problems arising from excess. In 1956, Leon Greenberg and John Carpenter, at the Laboratory of Applied Biodynamics of Yale University, turned their attention to the ordinary use of alcohol by the vast majority of drinkers. Applying the basic precept of social science, that no usage persists unless it serves some function, they sought to learn what needs have been met by the moderate use of alcoholic beverages through the centuries. These workers decided to investigate the effects of alcohol upon such traumatic emotional states as prolonged tension and sudden stress. An experimental approach was offered in the known relationship between the sympathetic nervous system and the electrical conductance of certain skin areas,[119] which is accurately measurable in levels of galvanic skin response.

A series of experiments was conducted with human subjects whose skin conductance levels were recorded through electrodes attached to their feet, and who were required to perform difficult card-sorting problems which created measurable levels of tension. At times, conditions of stress were created by sudden loud, unpleasant blasts of a horn. During these tests, various alcoholic beverages were administered. To discount any influence of taste, some of the drinks were introduced by a gastric tube directly into the stomachs of the subjects. It was first found that a man's emotional tension index could be reduced, producing a mild euphoria, by remarkably small quantities of beverage alcohol—as little as 90 cc. of burgundy or the same quantity of an equivalent alcohol solution. When larger (350 cc.) quantities of wine were administered, tension was markedly relieved. But with 350 cc. of the 12 per cent alcohol solution, a considerably less pronounced effect resulted, and in some cases tension was increased. With these dosages there was no interference with the subjects' efficiency.[120, 121] Thus the Yale scientists produced measured proof of the gentle and sustained tranquilizing effects of wine, compared to the abrupt and brief effects of alcohol. In so doing, they also presented the significant concept that wine has been utilized with beneficial effects by nearly all cultural groups for thousands of years, not only as food and medicine, but also because of its value in protecting man against the symptoms of tension and stress.

In this chapter an attempt has been made to trace, through the century following the introduction of the experimental method, the principal scientific findings concerning the physiologic effects of wine, in particular as these effects differ from those of alcohol. Only a brief summary of original significant research, conducted and reported according to modern standards, has been presented. Omitted are a vast number of published reports of purely clinical observations, which, although they tend to support the objective data, were not based on experimental demonstration.

That there is still much to be learned about wine, and about how to apply what is already known to the advantage of mankind, is of course obvious. But the book of the constituents of wine has been opened, and there is being accumulated a definitive literature on the precise effects of these constituents on human cells, tissues, and organs. It is now evident that, both physiologically and pharmacodynamically, alcohol is not the most important of these constituents.

Modern controlled research has succeeded in discovering, at least in part, why and how certain wines produce their diverse nutritive, cardiovascular, appetite-stimulating, stomachic, diuretic, and antibacterial effects, and how wine serves the deep psychological need of mankind for relief from tension and stress. These findings have already led to new and unexpected applications in the prevention and treatment of disease. There is already clear evidence that specific wines are useful as therapeutic aids in uncomplicated cases of diabetes, in simple anemias, in such digestive disturbances as the malabsorption syndrome, in the initial treatment of alcoholic cirrhosis, in minimizing acidosis in certain kidney conditions, in the treatment of anorexia, in relieving the infirmities and suffering which accompany old age, and in combating many of the diseases in which anxiety and tension are among the underlying factors. And it is now beyond conjecture that wine can play a major role in the prevention of alcoholism.

To the medical historian, it is of particular interest that science has now corroborated a great deal of the empirical evidence amassed during the four thousand years of the illustrious history of the oldest of medicines—wine.

BIBLIOGRAPHY

1. Bernard, Claude: *Leçons sur les Effets des Substances Toxiques et Médicamenteuses.* Paris, Baillière et Fils, 1857, p. 430.
2. Pasteur, Louis: *Études sur le Vin et sur le Vinaigre.* Oeuvres de Pasteur, réunies par Pasteur Valléry-Radot. Paris, Masson et Cie., 1924, Vol. III, p. 152.
3. Parkes, Edmund A., and Wollowicz, C.: Experiments on the action of red Bordeaux wine (Claret) on the human body. *Proc. Roy. Soc.,* London, *19:* 74ff (1870-1871).
4. Binz, C.: Die Ausscheidung des Weingeistes durch Nieren u. Lungen. *Arch. exp. Path. u. Pharmakol. VI:* 287 (1876-1877).
5. Kraepelin, Emil: *Ueber die Beeinflussung einfacher psychischer Vorgänge durch einige Arzneimittel.* Jena, G. Fisher Verlag, 1892.

6. Neumann, R. O.: Ueber die eiweisssparende Kraft des Alkohols. Neue Stoffwechselversuche am Menschen. *München med. Wchnschr. 48:* 1126 (1901).

7. Kuwschinski, P.: *Diss. St. Petersburg,* 532 (1888), quoted by Gizelt, A.: *Arch. ges. Physiol. 111:* 620 (1906).

8. Rabuteau: Contributions à l'étude des effets physiologique et thérapeutique de l'alcool. *C. R. Soc. Biol. II* (5s): 124-126 (1870).

9. Rabuteau: Des effets toxiques de l'alcool butylique et amylique (1870), quoted by Dougnac, F.: *Le Vin.* Bordeaux, Delmas, 1935, p. 131.

10. Joffroy and Servaux: Détermination de la toxicité des alcools. *Arch. Méd. Exper.* 7: 569 (1895).

11. Gréhant and Nicloux: Dosage de l'alcool que renferment le sang et les tissues après injection dans l'estomac de volumes déterminés d'alcool éthylique. *C. R. Acad. Sci.* (1899-1902).

12. Duclaux: L'alcool est-il un aliment? *Ann. Inst. Pasteur. 16:* 857 (1902).

13. Lombard, Warren P.: Some of the influences which affect the power of voluntary muscular contractions. *J. Physiol. XIII:* 1-58 (1892).

14. Quoted by Abel, John J., in Billings, J. S.: *Physiological Aspects of the Liquor Problem.* Boston, Houghton Mifflin & Co., 1903, Vol. II, pp. 23, 105-106.

15. Wendelstadt, H.: Die Wirkung des Weingeistes auf die Athmung des Menschen. *Arch. ges. Physiol. 76:* 223 (1899).

16. Abel: *op. cit.,* p. 106.

17. See p. 19-20.

18. Pick, A.: Ueber den Einfluss des Weines auf die Entwicklung der Typhus- und Cholera-Bacillen. *Zentralbl. Bakt. 12:* 293-294 (1892).

19. Sabrazès, J., and Marcandier, A.: Action du vin sur le bacille d'Eberth. *Ann. Inst. Pasteur. 21:* 312 (1907).

20. Remlinger, P., and Bailly, J.: Action du vin sur les bacilles de la dysenterie. *Rev. d'Hyg. 59:* 365-368 (1937).

21. Morton, H. E.: Alcohols, in: *Antiseptics, Disinfectants, Fungicides, and Chemical and Physical Sterilization,* George F. Reddish, editor. Philadelphia, Lea & Febiger, 1954, pp. 298-316.

22. Gardner, John: *On the Anti-Bacterial Properties of Wine,* paper presented before Amer. Pharmaceutical Assn., Salt Lake City (Aug. 19, 1953).

23. Masquelier, J., and Jensen, H.: Recherches sur l'action bactéricide des vins rouges (1953), quoted by Powers, J. J., *Food Technol. XIV:* 626-632 (1960).

24. Pratt, D. E.; Powers, J.J., and Somaatmadja, D.: Anthocyanins. I. The influence of strawberry and grape anthocyanins on the growth of certain bacteria. *Food. Res. 25:* 26-32 (1960).

25. Powers, John J.; Somaatmadja, D.; Pratt, D. E., and Hamdy, M. K.: Anthocyanins. II. Action of anthocyanin pigments and related

compounds on the growth of certain microorganisms. *Food Technol. XIV:* (12): 626-632 (1960).

26. Buchner, Wilhelm: Ein Beitrag zur Lehre von der Einwirkung des Alkohols auf die Magenverdauung. *Deut. Arch. f. klin. Med. 29:* 537-554 (1882).

27. Roberts, William: *Collected Contributions on Digestion and Diet* (1891). Quoted by Chittenden, R. H., in Billings, *op. cit.,* Vol. I, pp. 149-151.

28. Chittenden, R. H.; Mendel, L. B., and Jackson, H. C.: A further study of the influence of alcohol and alcoholic drinks upon digestion, with special reference to secretion. *Am. J. Physiol. 1:* 164-209 (1898).

29. Chittenden, R. H.: The influence of alcohol and alcoholic beverages on digestion and secretion. In Billings, *op. cit.,* Vol. I, pp. 137-305.

30. *Ibid.:* pp. 150-151.

31. *Ibid.:* pp. 154-156.

32. Kast, L.: Experimentelle Beiträge zur Wirkung des Alkohols auf den Magen. *Arch. f. Verdauungskr. 12:* 487 (1906).

33. Haneborg, A. O.: *The Effects of Alcohol Upon Digestion in the Stomach.* Christiania, Grondahl & Son, 1921, pp. 91-105, 113-114.

34. Franzen, G.: Alkoholwirkungen auf die Magenverdauung. *Arch. exp. Path. u. Pharmakol. 134:* 129-141 (1928).

35. Ogden, Eric, and Southard, Frank D., Jr.: The influence of wine on gastric acidity. *Fed. Proc. 5:* 77 (1946).

36. Loeper, M.; Michaux, L., and de Sèze, S.: Réactions du foie au vin. *Soc. Méd. Hôpitaux Paris* (Bull. et Mem.) *53:* 1212-1217 (1929).

37. Serianni, E.; Lolli, G., and Venturini, M.: The effects of solid food and of alcoholic beverages, especially wine, on the excretion of hippuric acid. *Quart. J. Stud. Alc. 16:* 67-85 (1955).

38. Carbone, John V.: The wine-cirrhosis myth. *Bull. Soc. Med. Friends Wine 3* (1): 3-4 (1961).

39. Althausen, T. L., Uyeyama, K., and Loran, M. R.: Effects of alcohol on absorption of vitamin A in normal and in gastrectomized subjects. *Gastroenterology 38:* 942-945 (1960).

40. Pavlov, I. P.: *The Work of the Digestive Glands.* London, Charles Griffin & Co., Ltd., 1910, pp. 109-110.

41. Carlson, A. J.: *Control of Hunger in Health and Disease.* Chicago, University of Chicago Press, 1916, pp. 178-180.

42. Winsor, A. L., and Strongin, E. I.: The effect of alcohol on rate of parotid secretion. *J. Exp. Psychol. XVI:* 589-597 (1933).

43. Margulies, Norma R.; Irvin, Dona L., and Goetzl, Franz R.: The effect of alcohol upon olfactory acuity and the sensation complex of appetite and satiety. *Perm. Found. Med. Bull. 8:* 1 (1950).

44. Irvin, Dona L.; Ahokas, Ann J., and Goetzl, Franz R.: The influence of ethyl alcohol in low concentrations upon olfactory acuity and the sensation complex of appetite and satiety. *Perm. Found. Med. Bull. 8:* 97-101 (1950).

45. Irvin, Donna L., and Goetzl, Franz R.: The influence of tannic

acid upon olfactory acuity and the sensation complex of appetite and satiety. *Perm. Found. Med. Bull. 9:* 119-124 (1951).

46. Irvin, Dona L.; Durra, Annemarie, and Goetzl, Franz R.: Influence of tannic, tartaric and of acetic acid upon olfactory acuity and sensations associated with food intake. (A note concerning the appetite stimulating effect of wine). *Amer. J. Dig. Dis. 20:* 17 (1953).

47. Goetzl, Franz R.: *A Note on the Possible Usefulness of Wine in the Management of Anorexia,* 1953 (unpublished).

48. Lolli, Giorgio; Serianni, Emidio; Golder, Grace; Mariani, Aldo, and Toner, Mary: Relationships between intake of carbohydrate-rich foods and intake of wine and other alcoholic beverages. *Quart J. Stud. Alc. 13:* 401-420 (1952).

49. Balboni, Claudia: *Alcohol and Nutrition,* presented at the symposium "Alcohol and Civilization," San Francisco (Nov. 11, 1961).

50. Engleman, Ephraim P.: Alcoholic beverages and gout. *Bull. Soc. Med. Friends Wine 3* (1): 5-6 (1961).

51. See page 72.

52. Benedict, H., and Török, B.: Der Alkohol in der Ernährung der Zuckerkranken. *Zeitschr. klin. Med. 60:* 329 (1906).

53. Neubauer, O.: Ueber die Wirkung des Alkohols auf die Ausscheidung der Azetonkörper. *München. med. Wchnschr. 53:* 791 (1906).

54. Burge, W. E.: Reason for the helpful effect of alcoholic beverages in diabetes, states of depression, and convalescence. *Science 48:* 327 (1918).

55. Soula, M. G., and Baisset: Action du vin sur l'équilibre glycémique. *IIe Congrès Nat'l Méd. Amis des Vins de France,* pp. 330-336 (1934).

56. Serianni, E.: Le vin et le jus de raisin dans la diététique et dans le traitement des affections gastro-intestinales, *Problema Aliment. 1:* 126-130 (1937).

57. Serianni, E.: Bevande alcooliche e metabolismo glicidico. Studio della glicemia capillare e venosa. *Problema Aliment. 2:* 21-29 (1938).

58. Weinstein, J. J., and Roe, J. H.: The utilization of fructose by human subjects and animals. *J. Lab. & Clin. Med. 40:* 39 (1952).

59. Lolli, Giorgio; Serianni, Emidio; Golder, Grace M., and Luzzatto-Fegiz, Pierpaolo: *Alcohol in Italian Culture.* New Haven, Yale Center of Alcohol Studies, 1958, pp. 77-78.

60. Balboni, Claudia: *op. cit.*

61. See page 38.

62. Carles, P.: À propos de l'action diurétique du vin blanc (1911). Quoted by Dougnac, *op. cit.,* pp. 108-109.

63. Saywell, Lawrence G.: The effect of grapes and grape products on urinary acidity. *J. Nutrition 5:* 103 (1932).

64. Fessler, J. H.; Mrak, E. M.; Cruess, W. V., and Hayes, J. J.: Die Einwirkung der Naturweine auf die Zusammensetzung des Urins und die Alkalireserve des Blutes. *Zeitschr. f. Untersuch d. Lebensmitt. 72:* 461-463 (1936).

65. Mulder, G. J.: *The Chemistry of Wine.* English version edited by H. Bence Jones. London, John Churchill, 1857.

66. Carles, P.: Fer normal des vins (1880). Quoted by Dougnac, *op. cit.,* p. 26.

67. Marsh, G. L., and Nobusada, K.: Iron determination methods. *Wine Review 6* (6): 20 (1938).

68. Amerine, M. A.: Composition of wines. II. Inorganic constituents. *Adv. Food Res. 8:* 186 (1958).

69. Lucia, Salvatore P., and Hunt, Marjorie L.: Dietary sodium and potassium in California wines. *Am. J. Digest. Dis.* (New Series) *2:* 26-30 (1957).

70. Gottlieb, L. S.; Broitman, S. A.; Vitale, J. J., and Zamcheck, N.: The influence of alcohol and dietary magnesium upon hypercholesterolemia and atherogenesis in the rat. *J. Lab. & Clin. Med. 53:* 433-441 (1959).

71. Lucia, Salvatore P.: *Wine as Food and Medicine.* New York, The Blakiston Co., Inc., 1954, p. 19.

72. Amerine, M. A.: *op. cit.,* pp. 174-176.

73. Hegsted, D. M.; Moscosco, I., and Collazos, J.: Study of minimum calcium requirements of adult men. *J. Nutrition 46:* 181 (1952).

74. Randoin, L.: Recherches sur la valeur alimentaire des jus de raisins frais et des vins, au point de vue de leur teneur en vitamines. *Bull. Soc. Scient. d'Hyg. Aliment. 16:* 464-486 (1928).

75. Randoin, L.: Vitamines, jus de raisin et vins. *Bull. Soc. Scient. d'Hyg. Aliment. 24:* 18-40 (1936).

76. Morgan, A. F.; Nobles, H. L.; Weins, A.; Marsh, G. L., and Winkler, A. J.: The B vitamins of California grape juices and wines. *Food Research 4:* 217-229 (1939).

77. Perlman, L., and Morgan, A. F.: Stability of B vitamins in grape juices and wines. *Food Research 10:* 334-341 (1945).

78. Hall, A. P.; Brinner, L.; Amerine, M. A., and Morgan, A. F.: The B vitamin content of grapes, musts, and wines. *Food Research 21:* 362-371 (1956).

79. Castor, J. B. G.: The B-complex vitamins of musts and wines as microbial growth factors. *Applied Microbiol. 1:* 97-102 (1953).

80. Flavier, H.: Évolution des vitamines B_1 et B_2 au cours de la maturation du raisin et de la fermentation alcoolique. *C. R. Soc. Biol. 130:* 499-500 (1939).

81. Cailleau, Relda, and Chevillard, Louis: Teneur de quelques vins Français en aneurine, riboflavine, acide nicotinique et acide pantothénique. *Ann. Agron. 19:* 277-281 (1949).

82. Ribéreau-Gayon, J., Peynaud, E.: Sur l'emploi en vinification de quelques activeurs vitaminiques de la fermentation. *C. R. Acad. Agr. France 38:* 444-448 (1952).

83. Peynaud, E., and Lafourcade, S.: Sur la présence de vitamine B_{12} dans les vins. *C. R. des Séances de l'Acad. des Sciences. 241:* 127 (1955).

84. Hall, et al.: *op. cit.*

85. Lavollay, Jean, and Sevestre, Jean: Le vin, considéré comme un aliment riche en vitamine P. *C. R. Acad. Agr. France 30:* 259-261 (1944).

86. Ribéreau-Gayon, Jean and Ribéreau-Gayon, Pascal: The anthocyans and leucoanthocyans of grapes and wines. *Am. J. Enol. 9* (1): 1-9 (1958).

87. DeEds, Floyd: Vitamin P properties in grapes and grape residue. *Proc. Wine Technol. Conf. Davis,* 1949, pp. 48-50.

88. Durmishidze, S. V.: *Tannins and Anthocyans in the Grape Vine and Wine.* Moscow, Izd. Akad. Nauk. S. S. S. R., 1955. P. Esau, abs. and trans., *Am. J. Enol. 10* (1): 20-28, 1959.

89. Durmishidze, S. V.: Vitamin P in grapes and wine. *Vinodelie i Vinogradarstvo S. S. S. R. 18* (2): 15 (1958).

90. Lorenz, A. J.: Unpublished manuscript.

91. Flanzy, M., and Causeret, J.: Contribution à l'étude physiologique des boissons alcooliques. I. Étude comparée d'un vin et de l'alcool. *Ann. Technol. Agric. 1:* 227-240 (1952).

92. Greengard, Louis: The pharmacy of vitamin B₁. *J. Amer. Pharmaceutical Assn. 1:* 230 (1940).

93. Fabing, Howard D., and Zeligs, Meyer A.: Treatment of the postencephalitic Parkinsonian syndrome with desiccated white wine extract of U.S.P. belladonna root. *J. A. M. A. 117:* 332-334 (1941).

94. Loeb, Oswald: Die Wirkung des Alkohols auf das Warmblüterherz. *Arch. exp. Path. u. Pharmakol. 52:* 459 (1905).

95. Dixon, W. E.: The action of alcohol on the circulation. *J. Physiol. 35:* 346 (1906-1907).

96. Koutateladze, Ivan Gregorivich: Sur la question du principal agent actif du vin de raisin. *Russ. Physiol. J. 2:* 1-14 (1919).

97. Vartiainen, Osmo; Venho, Eino V., and Vapaavuori, Matti: Influence of various alcoholic beverages on coronary flow. *Ann. med. int. Fenniae 42:* 162 (1953).

98. Romano, Carlo; Meyers, Frederick H., and Anderson, Hamilton H.: Pharmacological relationship between aldehydes and arterenol. *Arch. Int. Pharmacodyn. 99:* 378-390 (1954).

99. Morgan, Agnes Fay; Brinner, Lisa; Plaa, Colleen B., and Stone, Marcia M.: Utilization of calories from alcohol and wines and their effects on cholesterol metabolism. *Am. J. Physiol. 189:* 290-296 (1957).

100. Moses, Campbell: The effect of phosphorylated Hesperidin on experimental atherosclerosis. *Am. Heart J. 48:* 264-265 (1954).

101. Ribéreau-Gayon, P.: Le leucocyanidol dans les vins rouges: observations complémentaires. *C. R. Acad. Agr. France 43:* 596-598 (1957).

102. Tayeau, F.; Nivet, R.; Marquevielle, J., and Dumas, M.: Action du leucocyanidol sur le sérum sanguin in vitro. *Bull. Soc. Chim. Biol. 40* (1): 671-682 (1958).

103. Masquelier, J.: *The Components of Wine Having a Hypocholesterolemic Action,* paper presented before International Congress on Wine and Medicine, Bordeaux, France (September 26, 1961).

104. Balboni: *Alcohol and Nutrition, op. cit.*

105. Gréhant, Nestor: Recherches expérimentales par l'alcool éthylique. *C. R. Soc. Biol. 51:* 808, 946 (1899).

106. Mellanby, Sir Edward: *Alcohol: Its Absorption into and Disappearance from the Blood under Certain Conditions.* London, H. M. Stationery Office, Special Report Series, No. 31 (1919).

107. Haggard, H. W.; Greenberg, L. A., and Lolli, G.: The absorption of alcohol with special reference to its influence on the concentration of alcohol appearing in the blood. *Quart. J. Stud. Alc. I:* 684-726 (1941).

108. Newman, Henry W., and Abramson, Mason: Absorption of various alcoholic beverages. *Science 96:* 43-44 (1942).

109. Newman, Henry W., and Abramson, Mason: Some factors influencing the intoxicating effect of alcoholic beverages. *Quart. J. Stud. Alc. III:* 351-370 (1942).

110. Serianni, E.; Cannizzaro, M., and Mariani, A.: Blood alcohol concentrations resulting from wine drinking timed according to the dietary habits of Italians. *Quart. J. Stud. Alc. 14:* 165-173 (1953).

111. Lolli, G.; Serianni, E.; Banissoni, F.; Golder, G.; Mariani, A.; McCarthy, R. G., and Toner, M.: The use of wine and other alcoholic beverages by a group of Italians and Americans of Italian extraction. *Quart. J. Stud. Alc. 13:* 27-48 (1952).

112. Lolli, G.; Serianni, E.; Golder, G.; Balboni, C., and Mariani, A.: Further observations on the use of wine and other alcoholic beverages by Italians and Americans of Italian extraction. *Quart. J. Stud. Alc. 14:* 395-405 (1953).

113. *Alcohol in Italian Culture, op. cit.*

114. Lesanski, Edith S.; Golder, Grace, and Lolli, Giorgio: Relationship of personality adjustment to eating and drinking patterns in a group of Italian Americans. *Quart. J. Stud. Alc. 15:* 545-561 (1954).

115. Parreiras, Deció; Lolli, Giorgio, and Golder, Grace: Choice of alcoholic beverage among 500 alcoholics in Brazil. *Quart. J. Stud. Alc. 17:* 629-632 (1956).

116. Terry, James; Lolli, Giorgio, and Golder, Grace: Choice of alcoholic beverage among 531 alcoholics in California. *Quart. J. Stud. Alc. 18:* 417-428 (1957).

117. Lolli, Giorgio; Golder, Grace; Serianni, Emidio; Bonfiglio, Giovanni, and Balboni, Claudia: Choice of alcoholic beverage among 178 alcoholics in Italy. *Quart. J. Stud. Alc. 19:* 303-308 (1958).

118. Lolli, Giorgio; Schesler, Esther, and Golder, Grace: Choice of alcoholic beverage among 105 alcoholics in New York. *Quart. J. Stud. Alc. 21:* 475-482 (1960).

119. O'Leary, W. D.: The autonomic nervous system as a factor in the psychogalvanic reflex. *J. Exp. Psychol. 15:* 767-772 (1932).

120. Carpenter, John A.: Effects of alcoholic beverages on skin conductance. *Quart. J. Stud. Alc. 18:* 1-18 (1957).

121. Greenberg, Leon A., and Carpenter, John A.: The effect of alcoholic beverages on skin conductance and emotional tension. *Quart. J. Stud. Alc. 18:* 190-204 (1957).

Chronologic Index of the Therapeutic Uses of Wine

The origin of fermentation, especially of wine, antedates recorded history. Wine appears as a finished product in the pictographs of the tomb of Ptah-Hotep at Thebes

ca. 4th mill. B. C.

MESOPOTAMIAN CULTURE
(*ca. 5000-1400* B. C.)

Use of wine as medicine is illustrated by a prescription inscribed on a clay tablet at Nippur

ca. 2500 B. C.

The *Code of Hammurabi* incorporated legislation referable to medicine, wine merchants, and tavern keepers

ca. 2250 B. C.

EGYPTIAN CIVILIZATION
(*ca. 3000-332* B. C.)

Use of wine is illustrated in the medical papyri:

Hearst Papyrus specifies wine as a menstruum

ca. 1550 B. C.

Ebers Papyrus indicates medicinal use of grapes

ca. 1550 B. C.

London Papyrus specifies wine as common menstruum

ca. 1350 B. C.

BIBLICAL TIMES
(*ca. 1220* B. C.—*70* A. D.)

Use of classified wines as sedatives, antiseptics, and vehicles is illustrated in the Sacred Writings:

Talmud, written after

536 B. C.

Old Testament, written before

400 B. C.

New Testament, first recorded

ca. 1st cent. A. D.

ANCIENT INDIA
(ca. 2000 B. C.—1000 A. D.)

Vedic period: ca. 2000-200 B. C.
Soma, the supreme deity of healing, was con-
ceived as a being in liquid form. In the Vedas,
the healing potential of wine was made equal
to the power of Soma.

Brahmanic period: ca. 200 B. C.-
Use of wine in medicine is illustrated in the
Charaka Samhita.   1000 A. D.

ANCIENT CHINA
(ca. 1800 B. C.—220 A. D.)

Wines were incorporated in the materia medica
and appeared as menstruums in the ancient Chi-
nese writings.
Wine was used in libational ritual in the
Chang dynasty   ca. 1766-1122 B. C.
Wine was used in sacrificial rituals in the
Chou dynasty   ca. 1122-222 B. C.

EARLY GREEK MEDICINE
(ca. 900-100 B. C.)

Homeric times: ca. 900-500 B. C.
In the *Iliad* and the *Odyssey* wine was de-
scribed as antiseptic and sedative, and as a staple
food   ca. 850 B. C.
Hesiod described wine as nutrient and tonic   8th cent. B. C.
Hippocratic times: ca. 450-300 B. C.
Hippocrates used wine as an antiseptic, di-
uretic, sedative and menstruum   460-370 B. C.
Diocles of Carystus wrote on the use of sweet
wines in medicine   375 B. C.
Theophrastus described embellished wines   370-285 B. C.
Mnesitheus wrote of wine in "Diet and Drink"   320-290 B. C.
The Alexandrians: ca. 300-50 B. C.
The center of medicine moved to Alexan-
dria   333 B. C.

The judicious use of wines in therapeusis was stressed in the teachings of the medical school founded by *Erasistratus*   300-260 B. C.

Nicander used wine as the menstruum for his theriac   190-130 B. C.

Mithridates, King of Pontus, used wine as the menstruum for his antidote   132-63 B. C.

Hikesios wrote a treatise and commentary on wine, "De Conditura Vini"   *ca.* 1st cent. B. C.

Apollonius of Citium wrote on the medicinal value of European wines in a letter to the Ptolemies   *ca.* 81-85 B. C.

GREEK MEDICINE IN ROME
(ca. 100 B. C.-100 A. D.)

With the establishment of the Greek physicians in Rome, the therapeutic use of wine became a vital question. Physicians who adopted the medical use of wine were known as *Physikos oinodotes:*

Asclepiades, leader of the wine-prescribing physicians   124-40 B. C.

Zopyrus used wine as the menstruum for a mithridatium called "Ambrosia"   *ca.* 80 B. C.

Menecrates of Tralles used wine clinically   *ca.* 1st cent. B. C.

Celsus wrote on wine as a medicine in "De Medicina"   25 B. C.-37 A. D.

Pliny the Elder described therapeutic uses of wine in "Naturalis Historia"   23-79 A. D.

Columella emphasized wine as a medicine   4 B. C.-65 A. D.

Sextius Niger advocated the use of natural wine in medicine   *ca.* 40 A. D.

Dioscorides recommended wine for many diseases in "De Universa Medicina"   *ca.* 78 A. D.

THE ERA OF GALEN
(ca. 100-400 A. D.)

After the death of Asclepiades, independent medical schools were established.
The School of Eclecticism:

Athenaeus of Attalia taught that wine in small doses rouses the "pneuma" and restores vitality   *ca.* 41-54

Galen, first to classify wines by types and regions, and to recommend them for specific physiologic and clinical effects   *ca.* 131-201

Aretaeus of Cappadocia recommended Italian wines   2nd-3rd cent.

Athenaeus of Naucratis, the encyclopedist, recorded valuable information on the medicinal uses of wine in "The Deipnosophists"   3rd cent.

BYZANTINE ERA
(*ca. 400-700*)

Following the transfer of the Roman capital to Byzantium, the center of learning became displaced but the teachings of Galen prevailed.   330

Aetius of Amida detailed the medical uses of wine in the "Tetrabiblion"   502-575

Alexander of Tralles followed the tradition of the wine-prescribing physicians   525-605

Paul of Aegina recognized as the link between Greek and Arabic medicine   625-690

ARABIC PERIOD
(*ca. 600-1300*)

Arabic culture influenced western thought for many centuries after the death of Mohammed   632
and the conquest of Alexandria   641

The first apothecary shop established at Baghdad   745

The Precepts of Galen prevailed and the use of wine in medicine continued:

Rhazes wrote on the washing of wounds with wine   860-932

Haly ben Abbas discussed wine as a medicine in "Almaleki"   *ca.* 10th cent.

Avicenna promulgated rules for the proper use of wine in the "Canon of Medicine"   980-1036

Mansur the Great discusssed wine as a pharmacologic menstruum   *ca.* 10th cent.

Avenzoar adhered to and emphasized Hippocratic teaching   *ca.* 1162

Maimonides elaborated on the medicinal value of wine in "De Regimine Sanitatis"   1135-1204

Averroes applied Aristotelian teaching to medicine   *ca.* 1198

THE SCHOOL OF SALERNO
(*ca. 1050-1300*)

The first lay medical school in Europe established at Salerno   10th cent.

Arabic medical manuscripts brought to Salerno by Constantine the African   1027-1087

The "Regimen Sanitatis Salernitanum" illustrated the therapeutic uses of wine   *ca.* 11th cent.

Roger of Palermo advocated healing of wounds by second intention   *ca.* 1170

Ugo Borgognoni used wine as an antiseptic   died *ca.* 1258

Teodorico Borgognoni advocated the use of wine as an antiseptic   1205-1296

Salicet used strong wine as an antiseptic in surgery   *ca.* 1210-1277

Bruno da Longoburgo achieved wound antisepsis with wine   *ca.* 1252

Marcus Graecus published the first definite recipe for distilling wine   *ca.* 1300

Lanfranc lapsed back into the practice of suppuration   *ca.* 1306

LATE MIDDLE AGES
(*ca. 1300-1543*)

The physicians of the period began to realize the importance of the treatment of disease based on clinical experience.

Arnald of Villanova established the therapeutic use of wine in "Liber de Vinis" and popularized Aqua vitae   *ca.* 1235-1311

Henri de Mondeville advocated the use of wine as a "wound drink"   1260-1320

Guy de Chauliac used wine in the treatment of wounds and as a mouth wash   1300-1368

John of Arderne employed wine as a menstruum   1307-1377

Hieronymus Brunschwig ascribed miraculous healing powers to "Aqua vite composita"   ca. 1450-1533

The "Antidotarium Nicolai" printed   1471

Paracelsus stressed the tonic value of wine   1493-1541

BEGINNINGS OF MODERN MEDICINE
(1543-ca. 1850)

The publication of "De corporis humani fabrica" by Andreas Vesalius marked the beginning of an important era in medicine, an era which witnessed many departures from tradition and in which the foundations for the scientific age were laid.   1543

Ambroise Paré used wine as a tonic and to dress wounds   1510-1590

Richard Wiseman wrote on the medicinal uses of wine in his textbook of surgery   1622-1676

Sir John Haryngton published the first English translation of the "Regimen Sanitatis Salernitanum"   1607

Era of dispensatories and pharmacopoeias established by Valerius Cordus   1546

The history of wine and spirits as official therapeutic agents depicted in:

The Pharmacopoeia of London   1618
The Pharmacopoeia of Amsterdam   1636
The Pharmacopoeia of Paris   1639
The Pharmacopoeia of Spain   1651
The Pharmacopoeia of Brussels   1671
The Complete English Dispensatory   1741
The Pharmacopoeia of Russia   1778
Codex Medicamentarius of France   1819
The Pharmacopoeia of the United States   1820

The inclusion of many of the theriacs in the dispensatories and pharmacopoeias led to a polemic which resulted in the final demise of the theriacs.

THE MODERN EPOCH
(ca. 1850—)

U. S. Pharmacopoeia included unmedicated white wine	1863
The *Pharmacopoeia of Sweden* listed 15 wines	1869
Dr. Anstie published his comprehensive work on the therapeutic uses of wines	1870
Parkes and Wollowicz published the first study on the physiologic effects of wine	1870-71
Carles investigated the iron content of wines	1880
Buchner published the first comparative study detailing the effects of wine, beer, and alcohol on the stomach	1882
U. S. Pharmacopoeia deleted port and sherry under the influence of the prohibition movement	1883
Sir Wm. Roberts studied the effects of wine on proteolysis	1891
Alois Pick published his findings on the bactericidal effects of wines	1892
U. S. Pharmacopoeia deletes "stronger white wine"	1893
Krautwig and Vogel published a study on physiologic effects of various alcoholic beverages on respiration	1893-1897
Chittenden and co-workers investigated the effect of wines and spirits on the alimentary tract	1898
Wendelstadt published his findings on the effect of wines on respiration	1899
U. S. Pharmacopoeia, 8th edition, listed 12 medicinal wines	1905
U. S. Dispensatory listed red wine as a tonic, in addition to 17 other wines	1905
Benedict and Török investigated the role of wine in diabetic diets	1906
Neubauer published findings on the use of wine in diabetes	1906
Kast reported on gastric digestion and the effect of wine and alcohol on the diet	1906
Sabrazès and Marcandier published their results on the bactericidal properties of wine	1907
Pavlov demonstrated the appetite-stimulating effect of wine	1910
Carles reported on the diuretic action of wines	1911
U. S. Formulary listed sherry and 15 medicated wines	1916
U. S. Pharmacopoeial Convention voted to delete all wines	1916

Lolli and co-workers reported on the relation between wine in the diet and the carbohydrate intake   1952

Castor reported on B vitamins in wines   1952

Gardner presented findings on bactericidal property of wines   1953

Serianni reported on the effect of wine on the excretion of hippuric acid   1955

Hall and co-workers reported on the effect of wine on cholesterol metabolism   1957

Lucia and Hunt reported on the sodium and potassium content of California wines   1957

Engleman published findings on the relationship between wine and gout   1957

Masquelier and Jensen reported on the bactericidal activity of red wines   1960

Pratt and co-workers published findings on the grape anthocyanins   1960

Althausen and co-workers reported on the effect of wine on vitamin A absorption   1960

French Codex listed 7 wines   1960

Balboni discussed the role of wine in obesity   1961

Carbone reported on the relation of wine to cirrhosis of the liver   1961

Masquelier published findings on the polyphenols of red wine as a cholesterol-reducing agent   1961

Index